Learning the Language of the Fields

COWLEY PUBLICATIONS is a ministry of the brothers of the Society of Saint John the Evangelist, a monastic order in the Episcopal Church. Our mission is to provide books and resources for those seeking spiritual and theological formation. COWLEY PUBLICATIONS is committed to developing a new generation of writers and teachers who will encourage people to think and pray in new ways about spirituality, reconciliation, and the future.

Learning the Language of the Fields

Tilling and Keeping as Christian Vocation

Daniel G. Deffenbaugh

Cowley Publications
CAMBRIDGE, MASSACHUSETTS

For my parents,
in gratitude for their love and support

Published in the United States of America by Cowley Publications, a division of the Society of Saint John the Evangelist. No portion of this book may be reproduced, stored in or introduced into a retrieval system, or transmitted, in any form or by any means—including photocopying—without the prior written permission of Cowley Publications, except in the case of brief quotations embedded in critical articles and reviews.

Unless otherwise specified, scripture quotations are from the New Revised Standard Version of the Bible, © 1989 by the Division of Christian Education of the National Council of the Churches of Christ in the United States of America. Used by permission.

A section of chapter 2 first appeared in "The Ecological Indian Revisited," *Soundings: An Interdisciplinary Journal* 83, no. 2 (Summer 2000), and is used by permission. Sections of chapter 3 first appeared in "Defying the Tower of Babel: Industrialized Agriculture and the Future of Rural America," *Bridges: An Interdisciplinary Journal of Theology, Philosophy, History and Science* 8, no. 1–2 (Spring–Summer 2001), and are used by permission.

Library of Congress Cataloging-in-Publication Data:

Deffenbaugh, Daniel Grant, 1959–
     Learning the language of the fields : tilling and keeping as Christian
vocation / Daniel G. Deffenbaugh.
        p.   cm.
     Includes bibliographical references.
     ISBN-13: 978-1-56101-282-4 (pbk. : alk. paper)
     ISBN-10: 1-56101-282-3 (pbk. : alk. paper)
     1. Human ecology—Religious aspects—Christianity. 2. Stewardship,
Christian. I. Title.
     BT695.5.D375 2006
     261.8'8—dc22

                                                          2006022810

Cover design: Ann Delgehausen, Trio Bookworks
Cover image: Photo by Aaron McCoy, © JupiterImages Corporation. Used
          by permission.
Author photo: Turner McGehee
Interior design: Rachel Holscher

This book was printed in the United States of America on acid-free paper.

Cowley Publications
4 Brattle Street
Cambridge, Massachusetts 02138
800-225-1534 • www.cowley.org

Contents

Learning the Language of the Fields

couraged and affirmed within the context of a religious community if it is to be truly meaningful. In the concluding chapter, I will propose a means of recognizing the faithful practice of "tilling and keeping" in a new ritual for the local church community. Having been impressed by the Appalachian homecomings of my youth, I will suggest a variation of this observance as a complementary model for the celebration of the Eucharist. Of particular interest to me will be the question of why the early church never adopted the Jewish harvest feast known as Sukkoth, or the Festival of Booths. What have been the historical consequences of this unfortunate omission? A celebration akin to the Appalachian homecoming may be the kind of ritual that is needed in the church today for rejuvenating in a worshipful way our dormant ecological sensibilities. It may also effectively underscore our desire as Christians to live not in the hope of some future glory but as creative, redemptive, and sustaining "imagers of God" who engender well-being—peace, *shalom*—in whatever place we may choose to dig in and establish roots.

"Home," we have so often been told, "is where the heart is." Unfortunately, because of the mythology that has for centuries distinguished the Judeo-Christian tradition, our hearts have yearned to be someplace they are not. They have sought to "go home." The same can be said of our souls, those sparks of divinity that reside somewhere deep within each of us, which, if we heed the conventional wisdom, long to be released from the tombs of our bodies. Perhaps the old Appalachian hymn best represents our typical attitude: "This world is not my home, I'm just a passin' through." But this world *is* our home, and a few theologians have offered very compelling constructive proposals to help us realize this very basic truth. Their projects, however, tend to suffer from the enormity of their concern, that is, helping us feel comfortable in the cosmos. The time has come to narrow our focus, to bring creation spirituality down to earth and think about the many ways we can begin to appreciate, through our disciplined spiritual practice in place, the very real connection between who we are and where we live. The time has come to focus our attention, in the manner of Thoreau, on learning the language of our fields.

If we harbor any hope of putting aside our ecologically destructive and haphazard lifestyles, we will first need to acknowledge that, contrary to what we have heard in the past, our true home is where the *hearth* is.[4] That is, we can most adequately meet the divine requirements of our human vocations in the very concrete place where our food is grown, where our meals are shared and our stories told, where our ecological community is perceived as replete with personality, and where identities and moral commitments are forged from the very landscape itself. If there is anything we have learned from the confluence of Native American and European cultural traditions over the last few centuries it is this: that going home, our consummate goal in the past, has too often been a trail of tears; coming home, however, is in every way a path of the heart.

1

Spiritual, But Not Religious

Three Malaises

I have a friend who is a witch, or at least this is what she prefers to be called. A century ago she could not have made such a claim without serious repercussions, whether from the church, a town council, or a family doctor. But today she is one of a growing number of men and women who have forsaken their traditional values and turned to something new, something fantastic. Such seekers are often referred to as "New Agers" (by implication, those disillusioned with the admittedly dusty metaphysics of "the old age"), but this label does not do justice to the overwhelming diversity of movements that have exploded onto the American cultural landscape in the last few decades.

It is not uncommon these days to run across an Anglo man in an airport who has just returned from a sweat lodge and vision quest led by an honest-to-goodness Native American shaman. Many know a friend or at least an acquaintance who cannot start the day without consulting her Tarot cards or the *I Ching*. The ancient paths of wisdom are abundant and available. Prehistoric goddess worship, Buddhist meditation, neopaganism, yoga, channeling, numerology—all of these and more hold an irresistible appeal to many in our culture, and particularly to those under the age of forty. And for those of us who are at once attracted to such new ideas yet still feel a need to remain true to our traditional values, a question presents itself: Why this relatively recent interest in alternative traditions? What is it about the Western Judeo-Christian paradigm that has prompted such an evident exodus from the familiar to new promised lands? Why do so many prefer dancing around bonfires at the summer solstice, for example, to the customary rituals of the church? The answers to these questions are certainly complex, but one scholar has approached the issue—in a preliminary way, at least—with particular insight.

In the introductory chapter of his book *The Ethics of Authenticity*, Charles Taylor suggests that our postmodern society is characterized by three malaises. The first of these, as anyone familiar with the trends of the last half century might expect, is an excessive emphasis on the individual. Today the solitary person has come to be regarded as the final arbiter of moral value and truth. With the breakdown of the received ethical horizons of our past, it is now possible—indeed, all too acceptable—for men and women simply to establish their beliefs and commitments on a foundation of their own choosing and to be assured that their unique worldview cannot be legitimately challenged. In other words, a "facile relativism" has set in whose guiding principle is an extreme version of Polonius's memorable quip: "To thine own self be true." "This individualism," Taylor explains, "involves a centering on the self and a concomitant shutting out, or even unawareness, of the greater issues or concerns that transcend the self, be they religious, political, historical. As a consequence, life is narrowed or flattened."[1] Many today have no problem with the notion of "a majority of one," nor do they consider themselves integrally involved in or committed to a particular community. In good American fashion, they have gone the extra mile to pull themselves up by their own metaphysical bootstraps.

If extreme subjectivism serves to make an individual's life narrow or flat, then Taylor's second malaise ensures that this condition will only be perpetuated by a person's intellectual approach to the world. Since the Enlightenment, Western society has developed a blind faith in the primacy of instrumental reason; it is the principal tool to which we turn when we want to solve our most pressing problems. As Donald Rothberg has argued, the exclusive use of the scientific method in determining how our cosmos functions has resulted in a clear demarcation of three separate spheres, or "worlds":

> (1) the "natural" or "objective" world (known through the empirical sciences and manipulated technologically and instrumentally); (2) the "intersubjective" world of political, social, and ethical relations (known through open discussion, dialogue, and interpretations related to public action); and (3) the "inner" or "subjective" world ("known" [in ways generally not meeting the standards of other modern forms of knowledge] and expressed especially through the insights, intuitions, and creative activity of art, poetry, literature, psychotherapy and other quests for self-knowledge, and close personal relationships).[2]

Of these three, the one that can be known with the greatest certainty, or so the argument goes, is the first. Since the seventeenth century, a clear hierarchy has been established: through reasoned observation of the world, fundamental truths can be discerned and relied upon irrespective of their historical or geographical context. This reliability only fades to obscurity as one directs his or her attention to the social and psychological spheres. Unfortunately, in their quest for truth, many researchers apply the empirical method to matters intersubjective and subjective, often with tragic results. Factory workers in the United States, for example, lose their jobs and their livelihoods when the bottom line is not met; their lives are narrowed and flattened by the crunch of the numbers empirically derived. In the campaign to maximize economic efficiency, they become mere statistics in a cost-benefit analysis.[3]

Postmodern men and women, then, are caught on the horns of a dilemma: on the one hand, their individual values and truths are established subjectively and are therefore safe from the criticisms of others; on the other hand, their value as individuals in the world is easily and often thoughtlessly trumped by the apparently objective verities realized through instrumental reason. The human subject is nagged by the suspicion that he or she is really nothing more than just another object in the cosmos, a thing, because "in reality" numbers are more important than people and facts negate feelings.[4] One of the most basic features of our age, Taylor suggests, is this dangerous though pervasive reliance on abstractions.

Taylor's third malaise results from a confluence of the first two, that is, from placing the person who believes herself to be the master of her own moral destiny within a scientific paradigm that can so easily demonstrate her cosmic insignificance. Through the use of instrumental reason, industrial-technological bureaucracies have flourished, and with this has come the simultaneous limitation of individual freedoms. In the face of such monstrous institutions as Health Maintenance Organizations, for example, or transnational corporations, we tend to give much more credence to the validity of their "facts" than we would in most personal situations. We accept all too readily the social decisions made under the aegis of the empirical paradigm. "It is only good business," we say when the textile mill closes up shop in North Carolina and makes a run for the border. Freedom is lost in the sense that we feel helpless to do anything, and this only isolates us all the more. As Alexis de Tocqueville saw so clearly,

[a] society in which people end up as the kinds of individuals who are "enclosed in their own hearts" is one where few will want to participate actively in self-government. They will prefer to stay at home and enjoy the satisfactions of private life, as long as the government of the day

do not like seeing Bambi shot, dressed, and quartered—my sensibilities have of late turned to the wisdom of the land. I have come to realize in a very palpable way that, in the absence of natural predators, the deer population in Grainger County will inevitably exceed the carrying capacity of the community. When this happens, the latter surely suffers. When the dynamic balance of my place is jeopardized by the voracious appetites of too many deer ("locusts with hooves," as one of my neighbors calls them), the ideal of sustainability is threatened. Though I may not approve of its necessity or means, hunting nevertheless serves at times to maintain the integrity of a biotic community.

For many, this suggestion will be dismissed as entirely inconsistent with a genuine concern for "nature" or for the "environment," but I would say to those who object that they are not "thinking like a mountain," as Leopold suggested. They are not approaching the problem ecologically. An eco-spirituality that affirms the practice of sustainability as a means for manifesting the sacred will have to acknowledge that, in many instances, individual rights—the concept itself a product of instrumental reason—will need to be considered in relation to the goal of maintaining the spiritual and ecological integrity of a place. In contrast to the biocentric individualism of the animal liberationists, the perspective of sustainability might best be described as ecocentric holism. This maintains that the health and well-being of a place is as important as, and will sometimes take precedence over, the needs of those who are a part of it, whether human or nonhuman.[21]

Though conceived vaguely by some in our culture, spirituality can be defined as an intuition of an Eternal You who becomes manifest in a particular community through disciplined praxis. Eco-spirituality recognizes that this intuition can become uniquely incarnate in a place—that is, in a biotic community—through practices that have sustainability as their fundamental goal. I have up to this point said very little about the unique lens through which our sense of the sacred comes into focus: religion. In what follows, I will consider the obstacles that we must overcome if we ever hope to construct a specifically Judeo-Christian paradigm by which an experience of the holy can be recognized, affirmed, communicated, and nurtured. I will also reflect on the importance of spiritual exercise—in this case, the discipline of organic gardening—for maintaining both a personal and a communal sense of the Eternal You experienced in one's place. It is through this constructive engagement and theological reflection that I hope to provide a meaningful alternative for the ecologically minded men and women who at present find themselves resonating with the notion that one can and perhaps should be "spiritual but not religious."

The best place to begin this study will be with a consideration of the complex spiritual traditions that were for centuries the primary means by which indigenous peoples of North America centered their world and rendered it meaningful. My reasons for starting here are summarized effectively by David Leeming and Jake Page:

> If it is worth our while to be aware of the myths of the ancient Egyptians, Greeks, and Northern Europeans, it is just as important for us to be aware of the myths of the land in which we live. It might be said that until we know the ancient collective dreams of what we like to call "our land" and "our nation," we cannot know ourselves or be in any full sense a part of the land.[22]

In other words, if we are going to assume that the Eternal You becomes manifest in unique ways in particular biotic communities, it behooves us to investigate the narratives of the indigenous cultures of North America as a starting point for our reflection. The face of the land can be revealed perhaps most poignantly in the myths that preceded European arrival on this continent.

In proceeding this way, however, it will be important first to deconstruct the image of "the ecological Indian" that has been promoted by many in recent years, in order that we might reflect as objectively as possible on the stories and rituals that are central to many Native cultures. These narratives provide the rich, organic substratum into which our native roots will ultimately need to descend. Several questions will present themselves in this venture. In what ways has the holy become incarnate in this place, and how did indigenous peoples live in accordance with the values reflected in their creation accounts? Was there something about their unique mythology and rituals that enabled the Hopi, for example, to have a much keener sense of "the language of their fields"? The answers to these questions will certainly challenge our Judeo-Christian sensibilities, but they will also provide the necessary means for creatively addressing our own existential estrangement from our places.

Interestingly, though most of us have been sold the image of the Indian as a semi-nomadic hunter, wandering the Central Plains and living in a tipi, an agricultural lifestyle was characteristic of many Native cultures in North America—the Hidatsa, Zuni, and Cherokee, for example.[23] The creation narratives of these groups reflect a very profound understanding of the intimate connections between people and place, relationships that were established long ago in mythic time. These stories were often recalled or enacted ceremonially in the seasonal cycle of planting, nurturing, and harvesting native gardens. As we will see, the crops that these women and men cultivated were not viewed merely as impersonal commodities to be manipulated and utilized at will (an assumption all too familiar to Euro-American farmers). On the contrary, they were tangible symbols of a spiritual reality—a "mysterious Other"—whose presence animated the world and infused it with meaning. As I will suggest in chapter 2, it was this distinct sense of life's mythic dimension that enabled Native Americans to see and respond to the many faces in their place, and this perception was aided in part by the spiritual exercises associated with their gardening practices.

2

Children of the Earth

The Ecological Indian

Anyone who grew up in the late sixties will remember the promotion that started it all. A lone Indian dressed in buckskin paddles his birch-bark canoe across a tranquil lake. Coming to shore, he pulls his craft ceremoniously from the water. Before ascending a path that leads through a pristine forest, the almost mystical figure pauses to reflect on the beauty of his surroundings—the birds singing, the sunlight dappling leaves of oaks and maples, the smell of autumn in the air. As he turns to go, television viewers begin to hear the faint rumbling of something foreign, and it is not long before they discover what it is. Cresting a hill, the Indian comes face to face with an interstate highway buzzing insanely with diesel trucks and gas-guzzling cars. And then the coup de grâce: from one of the passing vehicles someone launches a paper bag filled with trash; it explodes into a mess of empty wrappers and discarded food at the man's feet. We are then presented with the image that has become one of the most powerful symbols of the American environmental movement: a tear trickling slowly down the rugged cheek of Iron Eyes Cody, the part-Cherokee actor who was cast in the role. The only spoken words in the ad were carefully chosen to

reprove the pervasive complacency of a rich, industrialized nation: "Pollution: It's a Crying Shame."

It is a truth of history that the victors often console the van-
quished with romance, and nowhere is this better demonstrated
than in the way that Americans in the late sixties came to view
both nature and Natives. Nature, once the consummate men-
ace to the thousands of people who explored and settled this
continent, had by this time been sufficiently subdued and dominated, whether through human ingenuity or by the presumed
providence of God. Children could now be entertained by Walt
Disney's harmless little "footloose fox" and never dream that
this creature's presence in their own backyard could mean no
eggs for breakfast in the morning or, worse yet, no fried chicken
for Sunday dinner. Wild animals had by this time become cute
and cuddly.[1] Similarly, Natives—who throughout American history
have been characterized either as sinners or as saints, depend-
ing on the prevailing cultural winds[2]—were now so statistically
insignificant that the nation that sought so ardently to eradi-
cate them only a hundred years earlier was resurrecting their
image in the hopes of averting an environmental disaster. The
portrait of the "noble savage," championed by the likes of James
Fenimore Cooper and Seth Eastman, was given a professional
makeover by the myth crafters of Madison Avenue and sold to
an American public prone to nostalgia. The image stuck, and it is
no less appealing today, as the proliferation of Native American
paraphernalia—everything from dream catchers to "authentic"
peace pipes—attests.

But how reliable is this picture? Does it truly represent Indians as they were before contact with Europeans, or even just two
hundred years ago? Simply to raise this question in today's political climate is to leave oneself open to accusations of blasphemy,
so completely has the icon of the ecological Indian been en-
sconced in our collective psyche. Attempting to defend the idea
that Native Americans were indeed true prophets of the land,
many will appeal to the very compelling speech of Chief Seattle,
the renowned nineteenth-century leader of the Suquamish and

Duwamish tribes of the Washington Territory. Upon learning that "the Great Chief in Washington" wished to buy his nation's land, Seattle allegedly spoke the words that would later be immortalized by scores of environmental advocates:

> How can you buy or sell the sky, the warmth of the land? The idea is strange to us.
>
> If we do not own the freshness of the air and the sparkle of the water, how can you buy them from us?
>
> . . . We are part of the earth and it is part of us. The perfumed flowers are our sisters, the deer, the horse, the great eagle, these are our brothers. The rocky crests, the juices in the meadows, the body heat of the pony, and man—all belong to the same family.[3]

If this is not a preservationist's manifesto, defenders of the noble savage will contend, then what is?

Most scholars, however, recognize that it is next to impossible to recover an accurate account of indigenous beliefs and customs, so thoroughly have Native societies been affected (or contaminated) by European contact.[4] What we usually tend to rely on, then, are mythical depictions that accommodate our own individual and sociocultural needs, regardless of their historical inaccuracy. The quote above is a case in point. Though it evokes a wonderful image of an exemplary figure speaking on behalf of the many peoples—human and nonhuman—who dwell in his place, the unfortunate reality is that these words were never uttered, at least not in the form in which they appear here. Ironically, the poetic narrative that has become a kind of ecological credo for thousands of environmentalists was written for a 1971 film entitled *Home*, produced by the Southern Baptist Convention. It is only very loosely based on Seattle's original oratory (if indeed there ever was one).[5]

Anthropologists like Shepard Krech contest the claim that Native Americans sought whenever possible to live in harmony with the land and that they were more keenly aware of the fragile balance of nature. In his opinion, the evidence to the contrary is staggeringly abundant. Consider, for instance, the late Pleistocene extinctions (10,000 to 12,000 years ago) of large mammals on this continent: an explanation for this phenomenon, Krech argues, cannot overlook the possibility that these creatures were simply hunted into oblivion by indigenous peoples. If this was the case, one would be very hard-pressed to maintain that the latter were aware of any delicate balance of nature. The impressive irrigation canals that once lined the Arizona landscape appear to tell a similar tale. Seeking to provide water for their elaborate agricultural projects, the Hohokum ("the vanished ones") who settled here (circa 800–1100 CE) were quite possibly responsible for the flooding, erosion, and soil salinization that eventually made their horticultural lifestyle infeasible. Unable to comply with the expectations of the land, they disappeared, leaving only their canals (now nearly destroyed by the urban sprawl of Phoenix) as silent reminders of what once was. Is this what we would expect, Krech asks, from a people living in harmony with their surroundings?

But perhaps the most damning evidence against the notion of the ecological Indian comes from first-hand accounts of early explorers who witnessed the brutalization of an animal deemed sacred by most Plains cultures. "[The bison] should always be treated with respect," Black Elk, a Lakota holy man, is reported to have said, "for was he not here before the two-legged peoples, and is he not generous in that he gives us our homes and our food? The buffalo is wise in many things, and, thus, we should always be as a relative with him."[6] Though these words resonate sweetly in the ears of those who want to condemn the wanton greed of nineteenth-century white men on the Plains, the stark reality, Krech argues, is that Native Americans were also prone to similar forms of sacrilege. The image of the frugal and respectful Native—the hunter whose vocation was a sacred art, who killed only what he and his family could properly use—has indeed set deep roots in the

American psyche. But archeological and anthropological evidence suggests a different story.

Take, for example, a site in southern Alberta known as the Head-Smashed-In Buffalo Jump, where the Piegan Indians and their predecessors—going as far back as 5,500 years—stampeded large numbers of bison toward a blind precipice and, finally, to their deaths some sixty feet below: "Buffaloes . . . would be stunned if not killed in the fall, and likely to break their legs and their backs. They and others driven into the enclosures that were still alive were shot with bows and arrows (and later, with guns), stabbed with lances, or smacked on the heads with stone mauls."[7] Today a thirty-foot-thick layer of bone and soil lies at the foot of this now infamous bluff. And lest anyone hold fast to the notion that every animal slaughtered was utilized parsimoniously by the Natives, Krech cites a number of sources to confirm the contrary. After observing one such jump in 1846, the artist Paul Kane speculated that "'only one in twenty [bison] is used in any way by the Indians,' and that 'thousands are left to rot where they fall.'"[8] Meriwether Lewis had a similar experience in 1804, when he came across decomposing buffalo carcasses at the foot of a 120-foot cliff. But perhaps most disturbing to conventional notions of the ecological Indian are indications that Natives would sometimes take only the portions of the animal that were most prized—the tongue or the hump, for instance, or even the fetus of a cow—leaving the rest to spoil unceremoniously where it lay. Apparently these practices were not as exclusive to the prodigal white sportsmen of the nineteenth century as many would have us believe.

Clearly, then, the romantic ideal so readily endorsed these days by those seeking alternative forms of eco-spirituality must be approached with some caution. To suggest that all Native Americans lived in harmony with the land, respected nature, and sought always to think in terms of "the seventh generation" is simply to draw on a tradition of "noble imagery that has generally had deeper roots in European self-criticism than in indigenous realities."[9] Therefore, while the focus of this chapter will in part be directed toward the actions and beliefs of Natives in centuries past, our conclusions will also need to be tempered by the very compelling research of Krech and others; we must acknowledge that, to some extent, we have been sold a mythic image that has been propagated primarily to mollify the spiritual yearnings of our own culture. I will not suggest, then, that what we need to do is merely adopt the belief system (and sundry totem items) of the Lakota, the Hopi, or any other indigenous group, so that we can affirm along with them that we are one with nature. This only obscures the complexity of both Native and Euro-American cultures.

Perceptions of the world cannot be transformed by merely assenting to a new, more enchanting set of intellectual principles, by deciding that "today I am going to think like an Indian." As we have seen, it is impossible for us to know the true nature of pre-contact Native American values. The best we can do is accept the fact that, for better or for worse, our Judeo-Christian and modern scientific paradigms will always to a certain extent be the lenses through which we view our world; we delude ourselves if we think that it can be otherwise. Yet our attraction to Native traditions nevertheless belies an ostensible deficiency in our received religious and cultural convictions; we recognize that Indians certainly had, and still have, something we lack.[10] Why, for instance, are so many of us willing to accept uncritically the notion of the ecological Indian? Does this reveal lacunae, perhaps, in our own perceptions of ourselves, our society, our world? Though the emphasis in recent years has been on the image of the "noble eco-savage" living in harmony with his or her natural surroundings, I believe the real, though hidden, appeal of Native American traditions lies in our present longing for a worldview that is informed less by instrumental reason than by mythology. Thus, an examination of the *mythological* Indian—one that focuses not so much on what Natives *did* in nature but on who they understood themselves to *be*—will provide the starting point for understanding, first, why indigenous cultures are so attractive to many today, and, second, what Native wisdom—insights drawn from many places—might inspire a kind of mythic rebirth in our postmodern age.

The Mythological Indian

The fragmented world in which we live and work—where distinctions can readily be made between subject and object, sacred and secular, animate and inanimate—has certainly taken its psychological toll on many of us. As the recent interest in diverse forms of spirituality has demonstrated, people have begun looking for viable means for putting the pieces back together, for taking what they perceive to be incomplete and making it whole. Many have turned to ancient or so-called primitive worldviews, most notably those of American Indians. But most seekers tend to speak in very general terms about the appeal of Native American spirituality, often overlooking the important distinctions that historically have made for such wide disparities in belief among these peoples. Those who have been captivated by the allure of indigenous worldviews usually cite one of a few very fundamental reasons for their attraction.

First, some have a vague sense that Indians represent the ideal that so many these days are trying to attain: they were—and to some extent still are—"spiritual but not religious." And in a manner of speaking this is correct. As Joseph Epes Brown has indicated,

> That which we refer to in our current usage as "religion" cannot be conceived as being separable from any of the multiple aspects of any American Indian culture. In no American Indian language is there any single word or term that could translate as "religion," as there is no single term for what we would refer to as "art."[11]

Even those who have relatively little knowledge of traditional Native American cultures can see that, at a very rudimentary level, the daily lives of these people were infused with a sense of the sacred in a way that ours are not. Everything from hunting to making pottery, planting to harvesting, was informed by an intuition of "the mysterious Other" that is simply lacking in our day-to-day existence.

Having said this, however, it is important to note that this kind of spirituality cannot be so easily assimilated into our lifestyle as some would have us believe. As any consideration of Native cultures will show, such a perception of the world can only take place within the context of a community that acknowledges and affirms the ritual quality of nearly every moment of one's waking day. The spirituality that is so attractive to many is nothing apart from a generally recognized worldview in which all things have their place, where every action is dictated, as it were, by clearly defined customs. Though the idea of "religion" may be foreign here, as Brown explains, there was nevertheless a wealth of ceremonies, rites of passage, and initiations that served to "tie back" a person's individuality within the Great Society (the biotic community). Yes, these people lived in a world infused by the sacred, but this mystery could only be encountered and addressed through very specific forms of "discipline." As we saw earlier, such impositions are not looked upon favorably in our postmodern era. Confronted with the whole truth of Native spirituality, most will turn to the cherry picking that has come to characterize our consumer age, accepting the worldview while ignoring the attendant rituals and group responsibilities that were an integral aspect of any Indian's life-in-community. When only a portion of the truth is acknowledged, the pieces of the picture remain fragmented, and the seekers go on seeking.

A second reason for the appeal of Native traditions lies in the perception that Indians were very keenly aware of the interdependence of every aspect of their world. In other words, they recognized very clearly that *who* they were was very much dependent on *where* they were. Apart from their unique surroundings, they were not persons, that is, creatures with a sense of wholeness and integrity. And not just any place would do. As the removal and near destruction of the Cherokee demonstrated in 1830, extracting these people from their land—where kinship ties abound and where rituals have been established with respect to the many "nations" who inhabit the place—was like transplanting a tropical orchid into temperate soil and expecting it to flourish. Spiritual starvation and exposure were as much a problem on the Trail of Tears as any lack of food or shelter, though not nearly so evident. The Cherokee were no wandering children of Abraham; the roots that reached deep into their native soil were sorely exposed on their march across Tennessee and Arkansas to their new home in Oklahoma. This kind of belonging is certainly more the exception than the rule in our society, in which professional itinerancy has become an accepted way of life. It is easy to understand, then, why the Native sense of knowing one's place is so attractive to many.

But *how* did Indians know their place? This raises another compelling issue that no doubt adds to the allure of Native American worldviews. As I have indicated, because of the almost universal use of instrumental reason in the West, we have come to feel disconnected from our surroundings. In our day-to-day existence we are less likely to encounter beings with unique personalities than "things" understood through a deeply ingrained filter of ideas and concepts. Indians, on the other hand, seem to have experienced their world in a manner foreign to us; their knowledge was immediate, acquired without the aid of abstractions. As Carolyn Merchant has suggested, in the early years of white contact, Natives may have actually *seen* a different universe than that of their Old World neighbors, for they alone engaged in what she calls a "participatory consciousness":

> In contrast to the transcendent world of Judeo-Christian religion dominated by the visual sense (illumination, light, seeing) and the mathematical, analytic world of modern science dominated by the disembodied intellect (mind's eye), participation precludes separation. In hunting for survival, the gaze is active and participatory. . . . In the meeting of like with like, distance as space between is

collapsed. Communication is direct and immediate. The objectivity that is dependent on distancing has not yet arisen.[12]

If Merchant is correct, then we may assume that Indians in pre-colonial times were incapable of distinguishing various aspects of the natural world as "other" or as object, at least not in the manner so familiar to us today. The faces they saw in their place were very much like their own: reflections of their essential self. To a contemporary American populace languishing in the impersonal wasteland of abstractions, this kind of mystical union, this belonging, is enchanting indeed.

Finally, turning from the dimension of space, some will indicate that they are drawn to Native spirituality because it affirms a much more naturalistic view of time. While we in the West today have come to think and live in a more or less linear fashion—always looking toward an uncertain future, sometimes running from our past, perpetually aware of the onward march of history—historically Native Americans seemed to affirm in nearly every aspect of their existence, and especially in their sacred rituals, the cyclical nature of the cosmos. "You have noticed that everything an Indian does is in a circle," Black Elk told John G. Neihardt, "and that is because the Power of the World always works in circles, and everything tries to be round. . . . The life of man is a circle from childhood to childhood, and so it is in everything where power moves."[13] But where does the power move in our postmodern age? In a culture in which most of us are oblivious to the waxing or waning of the moon, where the emerging darkness of evening is chased away by the fluorescent glare of climate-controlled environments, where the passage of time is measured by a numbered grid on the pages of a Sierra Club calendar, the power is lost. Yet deep in the recesses of our unconscious we long to know the power once again, to be plucked off the beeline of Western time and reintroduced to the circle of life. To many, Native American spirituality offers just the ticket for our return.

These three very appealing aspects of Native cultures, however, are unintelligible apart from the foundation upon which they were ultimately constructed: myth. "It would not be too much to say," Joseph Campbell writes, "that myth is the secret opening through which the inexhaustible energies of the cosmos pour into human cultural manifestations."[14] As expressions of the consciousness of a particular cultural group, myths provide the means by which human beings are able to render "intellectually and socially tolerable what would otherwise be experienced as incoherence."[15] In other words, myths provide humans-in-community with a working worldview. It has been a common tendency in the West, however, with its emphasis on verifiable facts, to malign archaic myths as simply ahistorical legends or "old wives' tales." As such, they are irrelevant to the concrete, existential needs of people living in the so-called real world conferred by the natural sciences. But nothing could be further from the truth. Myths are the dreams of a culture that, despite the particularity of their imagery (the presence of characters, for example, who are integral to the life of a place), are universal in scope. They are the stories that offer members of so-called primitive societies insights into the transcendental realm, the world of spirit.

In short, myths are like lenses that reveal the sacred to those who would otherwise be blind to its reality. In light of the three malaises of our postmodern age, it is imperative that we rediscover the mythic dimension of our lives. But the role that these narratives played in primal cultures is complex indeed, and it is not possible simply to adopt them as our own and thus open ourselves up to their significance and efficacy. There are certain gaps in our present perception of the world that will need to be filled if we are ever going to experience the full impact of these stories.

According to Campbell, myths serve four fundamental functions in so-called primitive societies. The first is mystical in nature: narratives concerning the creation of the world, or the journey and return of a culture hero, instill in the hearer a very profound sense that the cosmos in which he or she lives is an awesome place and, as such, should be affirmed and embraced in its multifariousness. At its most basic level, "myth opens the world to the dimension of mystery, to the realization of the mystery that underlies all forms. . . . If mystery is manifest through all things, the universe becomes, as it were, a holy picture."[16] Second, myth serves a cosmological function; that is, it introduces the hearer to the physical shape of the cosmos itself, though in such a way that he or she remains acutely aware of the aforementioned mystical dimension. Spirit, in other words, is not excluded from one's understanding of how the universe works. Third, myths function sociologically to support and validate a certain communal order. In contrast to the ideals of liberal democracy, where the needs of the individual are of primary concern, traditional Native societies were structured with respect to the requirements of the group. One was able to fulfill his or her commitments to society through participation in the rituals and ceremonies that accompanied nearly every aspect of one's waking day. Myths explain the structure of one's social world. Finally, these narratives play a psychological role: they allow the person-in-community to understand his or her specific purpose and significance in the midst of the first three spheres.

By contrast, in our society today we tend to think in terms of only the first and fourth functions of myth when engaging questions of spirituality, bypassing altogether the cosmological and sociological dimensions—after all, as we have seen, these are the provinces of the empirical sciences. The most obvious consequence of this orientation is a spiritual quest that, for all intents and purposes, concerns only the individual and his or her relationship to the universe: he or she can thus assume the feasibility of spirituality without the need of religiosity. Traditional Native cultures, on the other hand, lived in a world in which the cosmological, sociological, and psychological aspects of reality rested on a mythological foundation that affirmed mystery as a unifying presence among all three spheres, a single thread that drew them together. Their world was not at all fragmented or broken; on the contrary, it was supremely centered. Thus, while the

Indians of centuries past were probably not the proto-ecologists that many believe them to have been, they were nevertheless keenly aware of what Howard Harrod has called a "sacred ecology," which, when perceived through the lens of myth, rendered meaningful every facet of their lives.[17] While ecological balance may not have been on their list of priorities, *mystical* equilibrium was always a fundamental concern, and this is what we need to learn most from Native cultures. To this end, we will look briefly at two types of creation narratives, stories from this place that for centuries have served to "center" the indigenous peoples of this land.

Stories from This Place

What is striking about the cosmogonic myths of Native American societies is the way they typically fall into one of two types, and these, in their basic features at least, are not unlike the two creation accounts found in the book of Genesis (Gen. 1:1—2:4a and Gen. 2b—3:24). In one form of the myth, a lone deity surveys an expanse of water and resolves to create a world that will be inhabited by creatures of all sorts. In the second form, humans are fashioned in the womb of the earth, and from this primordial darkness they begin a long transformative journey into the light, passing from one form to another until they finally emerge into this world in their current shape.

From the outset, then, we can isolate two very basic points of contact—what Carl Jung would call archetypal images—from which we might begin a fruitful dialogue with the indigenous peoples of this place: first, the image of order created out of the chaos of primal waters, and second, the notion that all creatures were formed from the bowels of the earth. But before we can begin such a discussion, we must first recognize the very conspicuous dissimilarities between Judeo-Christian and Native American creation mythologies, because it is here that our paths and worldviews have diverged so markedly. It is in the details of these respective myths that we find, on the one hand, the source of the fragmentary lifestyles that most Americans live today and, on the other hand, the basis for the common Native perception of living in place. It is with the latter that we will be concerned in this chapter, saving a discussion of the former for chapter 3.

The first and most widespread type of Native American cosmogonic narrative is referred to generally as the Earth-Diver myth; it is found primarily among traditional hunting peoples like the Plains Indians, though it is not exclusive to them. The creation account of the Arapaho, for example, opens with the image of a solitary figure—sometimes referred to simply as Old Man—traversing the primal waters and contemplating how he might preserve his cherished companion, Flat Pipe. After fasting for a period of six days he concludes that "for [the pipe's] safety to the end, instead of being alone, there should be an earth with inhabitants, creatures of every description."[18] Crying out to the four cardinal directions, he assembles all the preexisting creatures so that they might help him in this endeavor. After a great discussion among the members of this group, the turtle suggests that certain brothers should be selected on the basis of their strength and agility to dive down into the water and retrieve from its murky depths a piece of land. Many attempts are made, each dive being more extended than the one preceding it, but no one is successful in reaching the bottom. In the end, only Old Man and Turtle remain, and the decision is made that the two of them should try to succeed where the others had failed. After transforming himself into a red-headed duck, Old Man, along with Turtle, dives down and remains submerged for a period of seven days. Ultimately, he achieves his goal and proceeds immediately to create the world, casting his newly found earth toward each of the semi-cardinal directions.

The symbolic imagery of this account is very important, for creation issues forth from the central primal reality, the Pipe, and spreads to the four corners of the earth. As Howard Harrod has indicated, "these images suggest an original integrity and interrelatedness of creation."[19] As the narrative continues, these characteristics are affirmed as each animal, in preparing this pristine world for habitation by humanity, offers herself or himself as an object of guidance for the future. Turtle, for instance, presents himself so that

> his whole body [might] represent the creation or the earth with all things; that is to say, the markings on the back of Turtle shall represent a path, its four legs typifying the Four Old Men or Watchmen (cardinal points); its legs or feet shall be somewhat red; by its shield are represented mountain ranges and rivers.[20]

Other animals and plants offer themselves as well. The White Buffalo gives his body for food and clothing; the Eagle contributes his feathers as symbols of holiness; the Garter Snake presents his body for the circumference of the earth. The offering of the latter is particularly important, for this image subsequently becomes the model for the Sacred Hoop or Wheel, a symbolic ritual object constructed from both plant and animal sacrifices (Badger, Cottonwood, Watergrass, Rabbit, and others are represented). This signifies in microcosmic form the intrinsic sanctity and wholeness of all creation.

What makes this myth significant is its various and abundant images of cooperation; they provide the paradigm by which the Arapaho and other Plains Indians order their perceptions of the world. These stand in stark contrast to our contemporary understanding of the cosmos and our place in it.

> The apprehension of the world by Plains peoples seems most fundamentally to be characterized by kinship. Solar/ lunar, astral, animal, and plant beings are not viewed as separate from the human world. Rather, these beings form a network of kinship relationships with humans and enter their world in powerful ways.[21]

The traditional Plains cultures, then, as well as other Native groups, regarded animals as possessing such traits as consciousness, will, and even supernatural qualities—after all, in contrast to humans, they were present in the beginning of time and instrumental in the creation of the present world. In some cases, such as the dream- or waking-vision, wolves, eagles, and many more of the earth's primal inhabitants became mediators of various transcendent powers. Thus the preservation of these vital relations through ritual activities was of utmost importance. The Plains cultures were exceptionally aware of their radical dependence on the earth and its numerous life forms. In a world where irruptions of the sacred into human experience were expected occurrences, they lived perpetually with an attitude marked by care, gratitude, and attentiveness to the world around them.

This is all well and good, some will say, and not too far removed from the popular characterization of Natives as ecological Indians, but care and gratitude do not explain the tragedies that occurred at Head-Smashed-In Buffalo Jump. From an ecological perspective this is correct; interpreted through the lens of myth, however, the story is quite different. When one considers the complex rituals that were always associated with the buffalo hunt on the Plains, one begins to see that the latter was no mere exercise in the mechanical killing of prey (the way that many hunts proceed today). On the contrary, it was in every way a sacred dance, complete with ceremonial means for expiating the human sin involved in taking another animal-person's life. These rituals, according to tradition, were established at the dawn of time, and, as ancient rites, they are the means by which the world preserves its original integrity.

Traditional Blackfeet mythology, for example, featured the story of a young maiden who marries a buffalo bull—a "keeper of the bison"—after he allows a number of his herd to be sacrificed for her family's sustenance. The girl leaves home and family to live on the Plains with her animal-husband, but her father, refusing to accept this turn of events, attempts to rescue her. Ignoring proper caution, he is eventually killed by the herd of bison. He is brought back to life, however, when the grieving and faithful daughter chants over a portion of his mutilated body. Witnessing this resurrection, the buffalo bull asks that the maiden also bring back those of his number who had

The affirmation of personality in one's world—beings with whom one can enter into reciprocal relationships and to whom one is morally responsible—is the first step that we must take in order to emerge as spiritual and religious creatures with a sense of, and commitment to, our place. But we will certainly not succeed if we remain addicted to the abstractions that have served historically to transform the persons in our midst into objects for exploitation. As I noted in chapter 1, our journey home must begin not with a single step taken from the realm of ideas but with an unfamiliar leap into a spiritual discipline that might eventually enable us to see faces where once there were only things.

Many these days take to the trails or to the rivers and lakes hoping in some way to regain a sense of being one with nature, but they fail in this because they cannot get away from the in-grained tendency to relate to these places as "environments," as commodities. The climber sees the mountain as an obstacle, a challenge; the hiker, "wilderness as therapy." As we have just seen, persons reveal themselves only in a relationship of care and grat-itude. The garden is one place where this can occur today, where people can, over a committed period of time—not just a Sunday afternoon here and there—listen and watch patiently, enter into alliances, perform rituals, give thanks, know intimately the myr-iad persons of their community, and experience a sense of living in place. Native American gardeners provide an attractive model for those of us ready to begin the journey home. It is to the vari-ous ritual practices in Native gardens that we now turn, hoping in the course of our examination to gain insights for our own spiri-tual practice.

The Corn Mother

Myths are nothing if they cannot be experienced and reaffirmed periodically, even daily. In other words, the language of myth must become incarnate in action if it is ever going to set deep roots in the lives of humans-in-community. Many are familiar with the rituals associated with the bison hunt on the Plains (which allowed the Arapaho or the Blackfeet, for example, to see the world through the eyes of their prey), but few have been introduced to an aspect of Native American life that, for many cultures, was as important to their livelihood as the pursuit of game. Many Indians sought also "to see the world through the eyes of a plant,"[25] and by so doing establish mystical connections between the welfare of the flora they cultivated and their own centeredness. Native American gardens were not simply plots of land where vegetables were grown as provisions for the coming year but places where relationships were nurtured throughout the cycle of the seasons. It is this sense of kinship, this affirmation of faces in our midst, that is most needed in our postmodern age.

Again, we should note that we are not examining Native American traditions in order to arrive at a better understanding of how we can be more ecologically prudent in our care of soils. On this level, it appears that Indians have little new to offer us. In surveying the ethnographic literature—books like Gilbert L. Wilson's *Buffalo Bird Woman's Garden*, for instance—we might be surprised to learn that Natives were just as guilty as any American settler of wearing out plots of earth, and they also were no strangers to the slash and burn techniques so often condemned today.[26] Gardens cultivated in the rich soils of river bottoms were usually abandoned after several years so that new soils could be farmed, sometimes just a short distance down- or upstream. Trees were girdled and brush burned so that the land could be cleared for agricultural purposes. And despite romantic images of the good Squanto showing pilgrims how to fertilize corn with a dead fish planted alongside the seed, Natives appear to have had little knowledge of the need to replenish the earth's nutrients periodically.[27] Indeed, the evidence suggests that Squanto himself learned the technique while living as a slave in the cities of England.[28] We have the ecologists to thank for what we know about the delicate balance of nature, the structure and content of soils, for example, and their relationship to the plants they support. What we are interested in here is sacred ecology. This will focus not only on what Native Americans *did* in their gardens, but on who they understood themselves to *be*: keepers of sacred rites and participants in a mythical drama enacted since the beginning of time.

When asked about the specifics of Native American agriculture of the past, most people are able to remember from their school days that Indian gardens were comprised primarily of corn, beans, and squash, the so-called Three Sisters. The first of these is a gift without which the North American continent could not have developed or flourished. Cultivated over thousands of years from *teosinte*, a cereal grass indigenous to Central and South America, corn played a vital role in the day-to-day lives of many Native cultures. And for Old World immigrants whose lives had been sustained by foods made from more refined grains like wheat, barley, and rye, Indian corn quickly became a central staple in their quest for survival on a new and oftentimes harsh continent. Despite this impressive history, though, corn today often carries with it a second-class status and connotation.

Among those whose spiritual tradition is replete with allusions to the goodness of wheat, corn has provided a ready metaphor for some of life's less desirable elements. Bad jokes are "corny," for instance, and a backwards country person is sometimes referred to as "corn pone." Many Europeans still turn up their noses at the thought of consuming the grain, regarding it as fit only for livestock. But *Zea maize* has for centuries been the backbone of this nation; without this lowly cereal grass Americans would not enjoy the standard of living that we have come to know and expect. Without corn, a priceless gift from the Indians, Euro-Americans would not have survived on this continent at all.[29]

Many Native cultures recognize and celebrate the supreme importance of maize in both their physical and their spiritual lives (not that these two can be easily separated). In many creation myths, corn is present even before the advent of humans and is often responsible for their very existence. The Navajo, for example, believe that First Man and First Woman were fashioned from two ears of maize—one white, the other yellow. Among the Cheyenne, corn and buffalo were offered simultaneously as sacred gifts to alleviate the hunger of the people. The Hopi recognize in the various colors of their maize—red, yellow, white, and blue—symbols of the four cardinal directions. In other cultures, corn is personified to such an extent that eating the grain itself is akin to what many Christians imply when celebrating the Eucharist: that life in all its bounty and beauty is procured only through sacrifice.

The Cherokee, for example, tell the story of Selu, the Corn Mother, and her two mischievous sons, who lived in a time before time. Selu's husband is Kanati, the first hunter, who provides meat for his family by retreating daily to a secret rock behind which all the world's animals live. There, he simply moves the stone aside, releases a deer or a turkey, and retrieves the prey for his supper. This fortunate situation is disrupted, however, when his two impetuous sons surreptitiously follow him to the place and accidentally release all of the creatures (this explains for the Cherokee why the task of hunting is now so difficult—men must search for animals hidden in the forests and fields instead of simply going to a special place and retrieving them). Hungry, the boys return home and lament the fact that they have no meat for their supper. Hearing this, Selu leaves for a time but soon comes back with a platter stacked high with wonderful cakes, the likes of which the boys have never seen. Curious again as to where this new food came from, the brothers devise to follow their mother the next time she leaves to prepare their supper. When they do this, however, they discover, to their horror, that the yellow meal they had been eating was actually flakes of flesh rubbed from Selu's body.

Convinced now that their mother is a witch, the boys kill Selu (obviously overlooking the fact that their food supply would also disappear with her). But like all good mothers, Selu continues to provide for her sons, even in her death. Before she is killed, she instructs them to drag her dead body across the ground seven times and to wait and see what happens. This they do, and the next morning the brothers are astonished to find stalks of corn sprouting from little hills of earth. The ears on these stalks, of course, contain the precious seed, the flesh of Selu, which will sustain them and all future generations, as long as great care is taken at planting and sincere gratitude is offered at harvest.[30]

In light of this story, it is easy to see why even today many Cherokee see the cultivation of their gardens as more than a utilitarian act for insuring the next year's food supply. They have for centuries known that their work among their plants is at every turn an entry into the world of the sacred. Spring planting is perceived not as toil but as worship. It is recreation in the most literal sense of the word: re-creation, a ritual reenactment and memorial to the sacrificial death of Selu. "Do this," the Corn Mother seems to say, "in remembrance of me." And at harvest, when the people finally eat the fruits of their fields, they cannot help but affirm that they are partaking of the very flesh of Selu herself. Human spirit thus meets the sacred through a ceremonial meal affirming that human vitality is gained through sacrifice and that the proper observance of rituals established from time immemorial will ensure another turn of the wheel of life.

How striking, then, the contrast between Native and Euro-American gardening: when the latter group sets foot into their fields, their myths, as we shall see, persuade them to behold an adversary; when Indians come to their gardens, their myths inspire them to encounter an ally, to expect an experience of the holy. Gardening for them is an act carried out in the midst of a multifarious community, for the garden is replete with personality, both human and nonhuman, and charged with mystery at every turn. It is the maintenance of a very tenuous balance of respect among all spirits present that ensures that health and well-being will prevail. Though Natives are concerned about the care of their plants, they are also acutely aware that sacred ecology must be their fundamental concern; sustain first the spirits of the place, and all else will follow.

In the Native garden there are varying levels of relationship, all of which serve to support each other. In *Brother Crow, Sister Corn*, Carol Buchanan illustrates these levels as a series of five concentric circles.[31] The first and largest of these represents the physical plane: the garden and especially the plants within it—corn, beans, squash, sunflowers. These are cared for by humans, who occupy the next inner sphere. Men and women, however, must perform a variety of ceremonies (circle three) to appeal to intermediary spirits—*kachinas*, for example—who occupy circle four. If the rituals are performed properly, these beings will then appeal to the spirits of the plants themselves (the innermost circle) in an effort to ensure the vitality of the people's crops throughout the growing season. Among the Hopi, then, when it is time for the maize to be planted, the gardeners will initiate a number of elaborate ceremonies to signify the start of the growing season. Men notify the chiefs sometime in February if they desire to have a rain spirit, or kachina (represented by members of the kachina society dressed in elaborate costumes), dance at the event and thus assist them in their planting. On the appointed day, the leader of the work party places his prayer stick in the field, while the kachinas (also spelled "katsina") remain at a distance "smoking for rain."

> After this is finished each katsina plants a few holes with mixed seeds, starting in the middle of the field, "because this part belongs to the katsina." The katsina then retire again to smoke and the working party finishes planting the field. At lunch time and in the late afternoon men and katsina race together to help the corn grow. After all the work is finished the group of katsina dances on the edge of the field. All go back to the village and the katsina dance again in the village plaza.[32]

The kachinas may also be present at harvest time, as Masau (a spirit associated with both germination and death) comes down from his cave and hides beneath piles of corn, periodically frightening and chasing the workers. What is important here is the fact that at both planting and harvest, as well as throughout the growing season, spirits are a very real presence among the corn, beans, and squash, and are regarded as essential to their growth and vitality. Hopi gardens are places where communion with the sacred is both expected and sought out.

Of course, Native gardens have also been the focus of less fantastic forms of community. Among the Mandan who lived in present-day North Dakota, the Goose Women Society was organized to take responsibility for the planting of the corn each spring. It was believed among these people that at the proper time every year Old Woman Who Never Dies, who lives far to the south, would send great birds northward as a sign for the women to begin planting: the Goose, Duck, and Swan were believed to be keepers of the corn, beans, and squash, respectively. Upon seeing these migrating heralds, the leader of the society, the Goose Woman, would have the seeds blessed by the Corn Priest and then organize her group for planting. Provisions would also be made at this time to cultivate plots for any woman who was unable to participate because of illness or feebleness. "The members of her society would come upon an appointed day and plant her field in a short time," Buffalo Bird Woman, a Hidatsa gardener, told Gilbert Wilson. "Sometimes a half a day was enough. . . . If we were invited to plant a garden for some sick woman, each member would take a row to plant; and each would strive to complete her row first."[33] This kind of care also extended to the poor and sick during the harvest: usually a public granary was established where each family would contribute as much of their crop as they could afford.

After the major task of planting was complete, the gardens—which for safety purposes were typically planted in close proximity to each other—continued to provide for a variety of social activities. There was weeding to do, of course, but when this task was finished (Native gardeners usually found it necessary to do this only twice a year), girls would build platforms on the northern side of some large shade tree, from which they would guard their plots from predators. Here they would often be visited by boys seeking out the attention of one or more of the watchers. Because conspicuous inter-gender socializing was considered inappropriate among the Hidatsa, the girls would usually goad or encourage their suitors with impromptu songs, apparently sung to no one in particular but in truth directed to a specific boy. From the tone of the lyric, the young man could usually tell if he had caught the eye of a particular young woman.

Other songs were also heard in the Hidatsa gardens, according to Buffalo Bird Woman: "We cared for our corn in those days as we would care for a child; for we Indian people loved our gardens, just as a mother loves her children; and we thought that our growing corn liked to hear us sing, just as children like to hear their mother sing."[34] And children were often part of the garden community: mothers would frequently educate their sons and daughters at an early age in the ways of cultivating and caring for plants. In this context, parents were able to pass on stories and reward exemplary acts or punish inappropriate behavior. So, from the start, most Native American children learned that they were living in a community whose boundaries extended well into the world of plants and animals. More importantly, they were taught that they had a specific role to play in the ongoing life of this community. "Even the smallest tots could place a seed in a hole and know they were helping to feed their people. This gave people a sense of being needed from an early age."[35]

Perhaps the most celebratory event of the gardening year was the Green Corn festival (sometimes referred to as Busk), when the hunger of the past several months could be banished with an almost unimaginable abundance of food. This ceremony usually lasted about ten days, as each family went about the task of drying and storing green corn for the winter. Later, corn was harvested in September, and it was at this time that the community worked together as a unit, with each family picking the dried ears and placing them in a pile in the middle of their field. Men from various societies would come together and help with the husking, an event that frequently turned into a competition among the younger boys for the affections of a particular girl and the approval of her family. "Of course each young man gave particular help to the garden of his sweetheart," says Buffalo Bird Woman. "Some of the young men rode ponies, and when her corn pile had been husked, a youth would sometimes lend his pony to his sweetheart to carry home her corn."[36] Here, the women of several households would work together to braid the corn for future drying and separate any ears that would serve as excellent seed corn. Enough seed was usually put away for two years' planting; if the next season yielded a bad crop due to drought, for example, the household still had a reserve supply for the third season. It was also in this manner that Native gardeners, usually women, participated in the process of natural selection that allowed untold varieties of *Zea maize* to adapt to a number of ecological habitats in North America.

By now it should be evident that communal gardens played a far more important role in some Native American societies than our received mythology has led us to believe. Though the image of the Plains hunter chasing buffalo on horseback has been predominant in the American psyche, the reality is that many Native cultures relied to a large extent on the cultivation of vegetables. And though we may not learn new methods of sustainable agriculture from the indigenous peoples of this land, we can nevertheless be made aware of a far more important notion, one that is lacking in the lives of most modern men and women: that the world is sustained not only by the principles bequeathed to us by the natural sciences, but also by a sacred ecology. Though we are entirely incapable of returning to the land and living the life of indigenous peoples, we can nevertheless acquaint ourselves with the various myths, symbols, and rituals that grew up out of this soil and recognize that these have played a role—though one that has been overlooked—in shaping our own identities. Further, the stories from this place can also provide models from which we can begin to challenge the received values of our Judeo-Christian tradition. In so doing, we might eventually unearth some of the neglected aspects of our own narratives.

Are there facets of our received mythology that might inspire in us a new understanding of what it means to be part of a sacred ecology? As we will see, there is a considerable amount of stubble and debris that will need to be cleared away from last year's fields before we can begin to plant anew in fertile soil. What we will find is that our current paradigm for tilling and keeping will need to be revised in order to provide an authentic and much more fulfilling basis for our ecological spirituality. But there *is* a land of potential abundance waiting just outside our own back door.

3

The Children of Abraham
and the Conquest of Eden

Last Year's Fields

Myths, as we have seen, are the primary stories of a culture,
the stories that shape and expose its most important framing
images and self-conceptions.[1] When writing his novel *East of
Eden*, John Steinbeck was aware of how the narratives of the
Judeo-Christian tradition informed, and in many ways determined, the lives of the first white men and women who settled
his native place, the Salinas Valley of central California. The tale
is strangely familiar to us: a wealthy man, Adam Trask, buys a
farm in a veritable paradise only later to have brambles and bri-
ars take over his once-fruitful fields and strangle the life out of
his closest relationships. Despite his most noble attempts to create for his family an Edenic wonderland free of conflict, Adam
finds himself perpetually embroiled in strife. Sowing the seeds
of *shalom*, his only harvest is a bitter separation of human and
land, husband and wife, brother and brother, body and soul.
The experience nearly defeats him but for the uneasy intuition
that his is somehow a universal story, arising from the deepest
recesses of human memory. Adam eventually realizes that, try

as we may, we cannot remove ourselves from the predominant myths of our tradition. They are like "invisible tails" that follow us through the courses of our lives.

It is no wonder, then, that *East of Eden* is considered by some to be an American classic, weaving as it does the archetypal images of the Judeo-Christian tradition into a narrative about a particular place. The stories of the Bible lend depth and meaning, tragic though they may be, to the life of the inveterate wanderer Adam Trask and to the lives of other immigrants like Samuel Hamilton and Adam's Chinese servant, Lee, just as they have done since those first peregrine Europeans gazed upon this new world. "The Promised Land," they called it, "flowing with milk and honey," a place where faithful pilgrims could finally build their "city on a hill." Such were the lenses through which Euro-Americans perceived their new home. But the grievous account that lingered just beneath the conscious surface is one that we have been most adept at fulfilling. This Steinbeck knew perhaps better than anyone: that alienation follows us even to the westernmost strands of the continent, that a malignancy infects our souls to such an extent that attaining earthly *shalom* is next to impossible, that we are merely sojourners in this place. *East of Eden* is our story too.

Having said this, I admit that it does seem ironic that we should turn to the Judeo-Christian traditions as we seek out more responsible ways of "living in place." As we have already seen, many of today's seekers have concluded that this peculiar heritage has little to offer, especially with respect to ecology. And when we survey the early history of the Hebrew people, another group of wanderers, it does appear unlikely that a concern for local ecology, gardening, and spirituality could be gleaned from the experiences of an essentially nomadic band of desert dwellers. Their recurrent unfaithfulness to Yahweh was more times than not attributed to the allure of the fertility gods and goddesses in their midst, agricultural deities like Baal and Asherah. Whereas worshipers of the latter emphasized the necessity of securing their place within the cyclical rhythms of the cosmos, the children of Abraham were intent on setting themselves apart from these idolatrous practices. The rituals of the land, though attractive on an intuitive level, only offered death and separation from God. So the early Hebrews focused their attention on a different realm altogether. As Bernhard Anderson has indicated,

> the uniqueness of the Bible is that it takes history seriously as the sphere of God's self-disclosure and of [humanity's] authentic existence. . . . Israel parted with the religions of the ancient Near East by declaring that history is the area of ultimate meaning precisely because God has chosen to make himself known in historical events and to call [humans] to participate in [God's] historical purpose.[2]

In the initial stages of the Jewish and Christian traditions, then, we find an implicit hierarchy in which the importance of sacred space (or, more specifically, one's place) pales in the light of sacred time, in which history is lauded over nature. And this raises a difficult question: If such a perspective has informed our values from the beginning, is our project not doomed from the very start?

A second concern follows upon this. Throughout its history Christianity has maintained a rather equivocal stance toward corporeal and physical reality. For example, despite explicit creedal affirmations of the resurrection of the body, many laypeople continue to assert that when a person dies his or her "soul goes to heaven," as if finally and forever released from Plato's "tomb of the body." This is only encouraged, innocently enough, by a popular prayer that many of us learn early in childhood:

Now I lay me down to sleep,
  I pray the Lord my *soul* to keep.
If I should die before I wake,
  I pray the Lord my *soul* to take.

Apart from the questionable wisdom of filling a child's head with thoughts of death just before bedtime, these simple lines foster an unorthodox image of how Christians should think about the hereafter. I do not doubt that many today still hold to the notion of an ethereal life after death, one free from the chains of material existence, despite the fact that this is contrary to what is stated in the church's earliest and most oft-cited creeds.

The apparently dichotomous references in Scripture to a spirit that is "willing" and a flesh that is "weak" (Mark 14:38; Matt. 26:41), or St. Paul's statement that "nothing good dwells within me, that is, in my flesh" (Rom. 7:18), only make matters worse. Christians seem here to be persuaded to think in terms of a qualitative dualism between body and soul (or by analogy, nature and culture), the former being only a hindrance to the latter. One is reminded, for example, of so many traditional hymns, sung especially in Appalachia, where the believer is encouraged to endure "suffering here below" in a world that is "not my home." And this is mild compared to the almost Manichaean way in which many preachers insist that God's creation lies hopelessly in the clutches of "the Prince of Darkness." If such is the case, will we not encounter insurmountable difficulties as we consider the moral aspects of what we have been alluding to as an "extended body," our place? Will our historical inclination to disparage physical existence prevent us from seeing the faces that rise up to meet us in our biotic community? Why should we even care about creation when we know that soon we will "fly away," as another hymn proclaims, to our true home "on God's celestial shore"?

Third, while our myths provide depth and meaning to the alpha of our collective history, they also have much to say about the omega, our future. This presents itself as another stumbling block. When we examine the eschatological beliefs of many (but not all) Christians, it appears that these only perpetuate the aforementioned qualitative hierarchy of history over nature, spirit over body, heaven over earth. In many premillennial Christian sects, the cosmos is viewed as little more than a stage upon which God's gracious and redeeming acts are performed. The natural world is not seen as having much in the way of real, lasting value, for in the end, after the cataclysmic events that will usher in the one-thousand-year reign of Christ, God will create "a new heaven and a new earth" (Isa. 66:22; Rev. 21:1).[3] What is alarming here is not merely an unstated depreciation of the created order but also the attendant suggestion that the downward spiral of history is indeed necessary for the fulfillment of God's plan. Even more disturbing is the implication that we, because of our inherent sinfulness, are incapable of being responsible agents in this scheme—apart from going out and saving souls, we must simply and faithfully resign our hopes to the will of a sovereign God.[4] This popular version of Christian eschatology only undermines the relevance of responsible praxis in one's biotic community. Why should we attempt to learn the language of a place that is ultimately not our own?

But the most powerful lens through which Christians have interpreted their relation to the world is the story of creation found in Genesis 1:1—2:4a and the subsequent narrative of Adam's fall from grace (Gen. 3:1-22). By now it is well known that the ecological wake-up call for theologians was first announced over thirty years ago by historian Lynn White Jr. in his classic essay, "The Historical Roots of Our Ecological Crisis." White suggested that, because of its peculiar theological and philosophical heritage, Christianity bears "a huge burden of guilt" for the environmental predicament of which Americans were just then becoming aware (thanks, in part, to Iron Eyes Cody). "Our daily habits of action," White argued, "are dominated by an implicit faith in perpetual progress which was unknown either to Greco-Roman antiquity or to the Orient. It is rooted in, and indefensible apart from, Judeo-Christian teleology."[5] Judaism and Christianity introduced to Western culture not only a linear view of time—in stark contrast to the cyclical view prevalent in antiquity and acting as the requisite soil in which the seeds of science and technology were destined to germinate—but a mythology that placed human beings at the center of an elaborate creation story. According to the tradition, God creates methodically and for a purpose: first the light and darkness, then heavenly bodies, plants, birds, fishes, and animals. Then, as if putting a final signature on a work of art, God creates Adam and Eve. Of all creatures, God made these last two to be most like God:

> Man shares in great measure God's transcendence of nature. Christianity, in absolute contrast to ancient paganism and Asia's religions (except, perhaps, Zoroastrianism), not only established a dualism of man and nature but also insisted that it is God's will that man exploit nature for his proper ends.[6]

As God stands above the world that God has created, so must humans also exercise a certain amount of power and control over their world, and all to the glory of God: "subdue the earth, and have dominion" (Gen. 1:28).

All of this is justified, of course, by the scriptural reference to Adam and Eve being created "in the image and likeness of God" (Gen. 1:28). Few theological terms have had an interpretive history as complex and varied as this one. What does it mean to be the *imago dei*? Interestingly, in the early centuries of the church, some attempts were made to include corporeal existence into the orthodox understanding of the term. Justin Martyr and Irenaeus, for example, distinguished between the use of "image" and "likeness," suggesting that the former in fact refers to the human body while the latter denotes the human spirit. This interpretation, however, found little support among later theologians, especially those well-versed in the nuances of biblical Hebrew. Other interpreters have suggested a more metaphorical reading of the term, drawing on analogies to known ancient practices in the Near East. When kings could not be present in conquered lands, for example, they would sometimes erect an image of themselves to remind their subjects with whom their loyalties should lie. In similar fashion, God erects God's image on the earth: Adam and Eve remind all of creation that God is Creator and King.[7]

But by far the most persistent interpretation, among theologians and laity alike, has focused on the human ability, in distinction from the rest of creation, to think, to use reason. Writing in the early fifth century, Augustine laid the foundation upon which most subsequent reflections on the *imago dei* would be constructed. Pondering the apparent dilemma of how humans could be, on the one hand, the image of God, and, on the other, made from the dust of the earth, he arrived at an opinion that would echo through the centuries:

> The former relates to the rational soul which God by his breathing or, better, by his inspiration communicated to man, meaning to the body of man; but the latter refers to the body such as God formed it from dust into the man to whom a soul was given that it might become a living body, that is, that man might become a living soul.[8]

Thus, humans alone can boast "a rational soul not produced from water and earth like the souls of other animals, but created by the breath of God."[9] Though Augustine did speak of original humanity as possessing both physical and spiritual qualities, he nevertheless established a clear hierarchy between the two, referring to the latter as the "better part." The body, of course, was henceforth known as the "inferior part."[10] Centuries later, Thomas Aquinas would reemphasize the importance of this distinction, claiming that "only creatures with intellect are made in God's image."[11]

Though the Reformers of the sixteenth century offered their own peculiar caveats to this definition, the fundamental understanding of the *imago dei* as primarily rational in character has remained a fixture of the Christian tradition and certainly had no minor influence on philosophers like Descartes and Kant, as they turned to the thinking subject as the sole arbiter of reality. Though theologians throughout the centuries have offered lip service to the idea that the human person consists of a unity of body and spirit, the primary focus has usually been on the latter, and this defined by the capacity to reason. Consequently, Christians have come to profess that God can be discerned primarily, if not exclusively, by intellectual means, by *understanding* the Word (*logos*) of the Lord, by *knowing* the truth that will set them free. The limitations of this orientation, of course, are evidenced in part by the conspicuous exodus of men and women from today's churches, some going to body- and earth-affirming spiritualities, others going nowhere at all.

Finally, with respect to humanity's relationship to the earth, we would be remiss if we did not mention what happened to Adam and Eve after the Fall, the single event that introduced sin and disruption into the peaceful repose of Paradise. As if our prelapsarian rationality were not enough to set us apart from creation, there is also the matter of an inevitable discord that is believed to exist between ourselves and the natural world. In contrast to Native Americans, who know that their gardens and peculiar places offer the very real prospect of entering into a relationship with the sacred, Christians have long held the view that, as a result of Adam's disobedience to God, a distinct enmity exists between humans and nature. Indeed, the soil out of which Adam and his progeny must draw their sustenance is cursed by God, so set in opposition to humans that toil and labor must forever characterize any association with the earth. In addition, women are now destined to experience travail in childbirth, and the Serpent (who in the Christian Scriptures comes to be equated with Satan) is doomed to spend the rest of his days crawling on the ground (as if this were the only appropriate place for Satan to exist).

Consequently, humans in their own acts of creation constantly have to rise above failure and adversity: men in their tilling and keeping and women in the act of giving birth. Our very identities are therefore rent with anguish and sorrow. Sin and pain pervade the world. The original *shalom* of Paradise was disrupted long ago by disobedience, and that brokenness continues to plague us today. As we mentioned earlier, this has also had an effect on the practice of agriculture; few in the Christian tradition expect to encounter the sacred in their gardens or in their place. One cannot meet the divine, the reasoning suggests, in an environment that has been cursed.

This, then, is the theological stubble that lay in "last year's fields." What is to be done with it all? When we consider the impact that it has had on the faces that rose up to meet our European ancestors as they settled this land, it is not difficult to see why so many today insist that it simply be hauled away and burned as worthless trash. I am not convinced, however, that this should be the last word on the ecological possibilities that our tradition provides. Like good tillers and keepers we might still hope that the theological remnants of former seasons can be composted, turned under and broken down in order to create life anew. But this only after we have examined the effects of our stories in this place and have determined the extent of the work that lies ahead. It is to the various ways in which the Jewish and Christian myths have played themselves out on the North American continent that we now turn.

Our Stories in This Place

Euro-Americans have always been great place seekers, but rarely successful place dwellers. The history of this nation features one series after another of settlements and dissatisfactions, of wearing out one farm to move on to another, perhaps in the next county, but usually farther west. The first European footsteps on New World soil had barely begun to fade before men were seeking out aboriginal wilderness tracks and animal paths and setting their courses for the next horizon. Soon the tracks became trails and the trails roads, with common names like "Zane's Trace," all leading to uncommon destinies, or so many believed. For these early seekers were lured by their myths, nearly all borne from their homeland, packed neatly away in their saddlebags and covered wagons. For a small group of sixteenth-century Spanish explorers led by Francisco Vasquez de Coronado, it was the fabulous wealth of the fabled Seven Cities of Cíbola, a vision that kept that company moving ever northward from present-day Mexico until it finally abandoned its quest in the desolate plains of central Kansas, with nary a gold nugget in sight. In the

ensuing centuries many would venture across their footsteps—
some seeking Coronado's quarry, others, like Mormon leader
Brigham Young, their own kind of alabaster city. But few along
the way cared to heed the narratives of the continent itself, the
stories that were shaped by its terrain and spoken by its many
inhabitants.

As Donald Worster has indicated, early European settlers
were inspired by two predominant though incongruous myths.
On the one hand was the belief that, being elected by God to
fulfill God's sovereign purposes, they could somehow recover
Eden in all its innocence and, by association with such a place,
lead lives free of corruption and pleasing to their maker. On
the other hand was the historically subsequent idea that their
own enlightened self-interests, unhindered by any external laws
or regulations (for, after all, these are unnecessary in Paradise),
could actually transform the vice of greed into a veritable virtue. Such have been the dual themes resonating at the core of
the American psyche:

> Regaining paradise is an ancient, wonderful dream, and
> the Edenic dream and the Edenic nature that inspired it
> are the most wonderful things about America. They ex-
> plain why we are a nation of idealists. They explain the
> fact that we are an avid group of nature lovers. . . . [But]
> we have also been a nation of consummate nature destroy-
> ers, perhaps the most destructive ever; and again it has
> been the dream of living innocently in a bountiful Eden
> that has been responsible. Innocence, no matter how con-
> trived or willful, can, after all, produce tragedy.[12]

History may have been quite different, however, had the
Europeans who first settled this continent arrived with less of
a sense of power and *noblesse oblige* and more of an inclination
toward the Christian virtues of humility and compassion. They
could have learned much more from Natives about dwelling in
this place than they were willing to admit. Despite wonderful

legends that every schoolchild learns extolling the pristine beauty of the "virgin land" that greeted the likes of Captain John Smith or Governor John Winthrop, North America had been well taken care of—managed, if you will—by Native cultures centuries before the arrival of the colonists. The wilderness that so terrified and confederated the members of the Massachusetts Bay Colony in the 1630s was hardly the wild and chaotic place that Puritan preachers like John Cotton and Richard Mather believed it to be. As William Cronon suggests in *Changes in the Land*, a study of the ecological transformations that took place in New England during the early colonial period, Native Americans had long imposed their own order on the place that was their home. But Europeans lacked the insight and the inclination to recognize it for what it was. The Indians of the New World had a different manner of relating to their environment. They told different stories.[13]

Perhaps the most puzzling aspect of Native American life from the perspective of the European immigrants was what the latter perceived to be a perpetual life of poverty in the midst of plenty. "Here was a riddle: how could a land be so rich and its people so poor? At least in the eyes of many colonists, the Indians, blessed with such great natural wealth, lived 'like to our Beggers in England.'"[14] But such a perception only illustrates the extent to which the colonists, in their presumed position of privilege and power, were unable to affirm anything but their own worldview. They took pity on "the savages" and took advantage of them, all with an air of exceeding condescension. For what intelligent person, they reasoned, would willfully choose a life as debased as that of these poor creatures? The Natives' apparent disregard for the concerns of the morrow kept their small communities constantly on the move, and such mobility (as any reading of the Exodus narrative will remind us) was a certain sign of waywardness. (When making this assessment, the colonists apparently ignored their own wanderings.)

While the children of Abraham remained relatively sedentary in their New England homes and villages, the Indians of the region seemed perpetually to be shifting their places of habitation. In the spring they made their camps at the rivers to take advantage of the spawning alewives, sturgeon, and salmon, and to plant their crops of corn, beans, and squash in the nearby forest clearings. In the autumn months they would break up into smaller family bands and move inland to hunt beaver, caribou, moose, and deer. Often in late winter, or when the lack of snow made tracking animals impossible, there would be protracted periods of scarcity and hunger, a condition that many Indians appeared to accept without complaint, even with cheerfulness. To the European sensibility this smacked of sheer ignorance: Why did these people not prepare for such conditions, perhaps by storing up enough provisions and remaining in a fixed location during these harsh starving times? Why go hungry when it could so easily be avoided? The colonists could only draw one conclusion: these creatures were subhuman, unable to think things through, or just plain lazy. Their lack of thrift and industry certainly excluded them from the community of God's elect.

The distinctive manner in which Native Americans experienced and knew their world was entirely lost on the colonists. In contrast to indigenous stories that made the Indians especially aware of their responsibilities to their larger biotic community, the newly arrived Europeans lived narratives that seemed only to promote a consciousness of conquest. They were, after all, the *imago dei*, transcendent over, not subject to, the vicissitudes of nature. Also by this time in Western Europe, any immediate knowledge of the world—based on touch, for example, or the other base senses that appeared to be so prevalent among the Natives—had become altogether suspect. It is not the body that knows; truth is gained through objective observation and ratiocination. Only thus can Plato's forms, or God's will, be known. This perspective served only to remove the colonists yet another step from their natural surroundings and from their indigenous neighbors. As Carolyn Merchant has suggested, "vision as the primary source of knowledge creates an observer distant from nature. Knowledge gained through the body by touch, smell, and taste is degraded in favor of knowledge modeled on perspective. A distant God is substituted for the spirits within animals, trees, and fetishes."[15] Value, therefore, has to be ascribed rather than experienced face-to-face, and ascribing value was what most of the colonists were all about.

Having arrived from lands that for centuries had experienced the paranoid persecutions of alleged pagans—witches and warlocks who reputedly stole away to the deepest forests on moonlit nights to perform their sordid satanic rituals[16]—these immigrants were none too sympathetic toward Natives whose interpretation of the natural world so often featured the appeasement of spirits and "animal masters." To many, it was Canaan and its fertility deities all over again. With the hobgoblins effectively driven from the British Isles, and off European soil, the colonists went to great lengths to ensure that no such puckish spirits, or worse, would encroach upon their newfound domain, their Eden. Satan was to be routed out of every inch of wilderness that surrounded and threatened to engulf their small villages. Forests were to be cleared and gardens established with rows of crops so neat and orderly as to be pleasing to the Lord.

Nowhere was the suggestion heard that such an undertaking might displease the spirits of the places themselves or create a blemish on the face of the land. For in the words of Wendell Berry, the colonists came "with visions of former places but not [with] the sight to see where [they were],"[17] and where they had been was a region of scarcity in which such common necessities as firewood and arable farm land could be acquired only at a premium price. No perceived spiritual essence in their new home could begin to overwhelm a lifetime of desire for the provisions that had hitherto been inaccessible, beyond their grasp. They rather preferred living in a disenchanted cosmos, one in which their quest for prosperity and Edenic abundance was unhindered by any moral constraints. So, where the Indians saw persons and a sacred ecology, the immigrants tended only to see provisions and potential profit.

Thus began the commodification of nature in America, an objectification of the land that had long been regarded by Natives as a source of value and meaning. And accompanying this attitude was the inevitable disregard for the mythological and ecological relations of the various commodities to their particular places. Trees and animals, rivers and meadows all became functionally and spiritually disconnected from the habitat in which they played an often indispensable role. This perspective was only possible among a people who considered themselves removed from the landscape, who could approach it only conceptually.

One abstraction that colonists imposed upon the Natives' homeland was a multitude of new and, to the Indians' way of thinking, arbitrarily chosen names. Regions of the landscape that had previously been known simply by their peculiar ecological or geographical features were now shackled with such anomalous appellations as "Plymouth" or "New Haven," words that seemed to bespeak allegiances to domains far removed from the ones at hand. And with this nominal acquisition of place came its more concrete corollary, an idea that had been altogether foreign to Native Americans until this time: the concept of land as capital, an investment. In contrast to the Natives, who had always perceived themselves as belonging to a particular place, the new immigrants wasted little time in demonstrating the belief that one place or another could actually belong to them. Of course, all of this was justified by a theology uniquely suited to the rigors of imperialistic conquest. As the Judeo-Christian God placed Adam and Eve in the Garden to have dominion, so could land be exacted as rightful property by anyone willing to heed the divine call to make such "improvements" as were necessary to merit the name of good stewardship. The latter was determined solely by means of productivity; the person whose labors in the wilderness bore fruit in season could be said to own the land that yielded such provisions, its value having been enhanced in the eyes of God. By contrast, Native Americans, who appeared to the colonists to lack any kind of industrious work ethic, could thereby hold no legitimate claim to their places. They were lazy and unambitious, as demonstrated by their perpetual poverty.

So places became plots, and all with the blessing of a Puritan God, who, it should be noted, was another import. Property, which in former lands had been quite scarce, was now seen as the one commodity that could assure a man and his family of a potentially lucrative vocation here on earth, as well as a place among the righteous in the kingdom of heaven. And the means by which these parcels were distributed appeared to be as arbitrary as the names they were eventually given. The Natives were able to recognize certain communal boundaries and natural regions based upon how these places had been utilized by groups in the past—wood lots and cornfields, for example. But the immigrants were obviously working under different assumptions. As Cronon indicates,

> once transferred into private hands . . . most such lands became abstract parcels whose legal definition bore no inherent relation to their use: a person owned everything on them, not just specific activities which could be conducted within their boundaries. Whereas the earliest deeds tended to describe land in terms of its topography and use—for instance, as the mowing field between two certain creeks—later deeds described land in terms of lots held by adjacent owners, and marked territories using the surveyor's abstractions of points of the compass and metes and bounds.[18]

To the Natives who inhabited this place, such assessments must have seemed both sacrilegious and absurd, but the colonists were uninterested in their opinions. Indeed, after several decades of acquisition by improvement, the Indians themselves came to be regarded as troublesome intruders, a nuisance (their gardens along the rivers, for example, prevented cows and other domestic livestock from grazing without encumbrance or conflict). Those few who did survive the grim ravishes of small pox eventually found themselves either assimilated into a culture that refused to recognize any aspect of their former existence or driven farther west to places whose indigenous myths and rituals were alien to their unique manner of thinking and being in their original habitat. Invariably, the lands on which Native people were placed were as arid and infertile as any on the continent, and when they refused or were unable to make their own improvements on these, it was all too easy to justify the appropriation of their real estate for white settlers willing to make a good Christian go of it.

To add one final insult to scores of past injuries, in 1887 Congress approved the Dawes Severalty Act, legislation meant to be conciliatory toward Native people, but so short-sighted as to be absurd and thus entirely ineffective. It was ultimately destructive to traditional ways of life in most Native American communities. By order of the U.S. government, Indian families, like so many white immigrants before them, were given 160-acre parcels of land and told to make a profit, as the white man's God required. They were encouraged to find their own Eden beyond the hundredth meridian, the so-called dry line that divides the central United States between the agricultural haves and have-nots. Thus, with the stroke of a pen in Washington, the tradition of communal gardening among Natives—usually done by women—was effectively replaced by tractors and plows and Indian men planting and harvesting huge fields of wheat or corn. The understanding was that this would be done not in community, as they had known for untold generations, but individually. They were now to be good yeoman farmers. Seed-saving, garden songs and rituals, dancing to the spirits of a place, mythological narratives—all of these were to be replaced by the values and technology of the modern age, and all for the good of the Indian.

From the start, this apparently well-intentioned legislation was doomed to failure. Congress, like the rest of the country, had severely misjudged the very real differences between the Native and Euro-American worldviews.

The Dawes Severalty Act . . . thrust the Indian into a monetary economy without providing them with the technological, educational, scientific, and monetary means to survive in it. As a result, the Indians sold or leased their land, because they could not farm it profitably or because the land was infertile or subject to a level of taxation that they could not pay.[19]

Sadly, by the early decades of the twentieth century, memories of Native gardening were quickly fading, maintained only among the most traditional Indians, like the Hidatsa gardener Buffalo Bird Woman. Also by this time, most government officials, like most Americans, had given up on the apparently lazy Indian. Displaced tribes were now destined to live the remainder of their communal lives on poverty-stricken reservations, in conditions far removed from the noble image that would later be resurrected to stem the tide of a burgeoning environmental crisis. Only then would these sinners of nearly a century past become national saints.

The commodification of nature was achieved at the hands of colonists whose worldview would not allow them to see the face of the places they inhabited or to recognize the legitimacy of aboriginal customs and perspectives. Like so many of their European predecessors, they proceeded by abstractions when assessing value in their world. This denial of the persons so plainly in their midst—whether human, animal, or plant—enabled their aspiring economic pursuits to proceed unabated and served also to initiate the palpable crucifixion of the land, that is, the methodical annihilation of a place that was believed originally to be their salvation. Nowhere was this more poignantly realized than on the Great Plains of the central United States. Here, history demonstrated the inevitable result of a people driven by wonderful myths of recovering Eden while simultaneously abstracting themselves from any perceived moral obligation to their biotic community.

What Happened to the Garden?

The Dust Bowl of the 1930s was one of America's most tragic environmental disasters. The event exacted both an ecological and a human toll on a landscape that many to this day consider too bland and desolate to be of any particular value, a region extending from the panhandles of Texas and Oklahoma to western Kansas and portions of Colorado. Present-day travelers usually lament their long trips across the Kansas or Nebraska flatlands on their way to some more appealing destination like the Rocky Mountains. But apart from the biological diversity present here, from the rich varieties of soil to the abundance of prairie plant species, the southern Plains also intimate past stories of the best laid schemes of mice and men gone awry, accounts that should not be easily forgotten or hurried through on the way to some majestic mountain vista. It is difficult to find a more instructive illustration of what happens when human beings blinded by ambition refuse to acknowledge the expectations of the land.

In *Dust Bowl*, a study of the environmental history of this area, Donald Worster offers an insightful reading of the human migrations and agricultural practices that ultimately led to a decade of disastrous dust storms, an era commonly referred to by Plains locals as "the dirty thirties." When the Homestead Act of 1862 gave more adventurous (or perhaps more desperate) Americans the opportunity to own a 160-acre tract of western land merely for the price of its improvement, many jumped at the chance, and the land rush of the latter half of the nineteenth century was under way. In a matter of a few short decades the western prairies—which had hitherto known only the heavy-hooved grazings of massive buffalo herds and the less conspicuous footsteps of the Plains Indian hunters who followed in their wake—were now suffering under the expansionistic passions of immigrant fortune-seekers, a phenomenon that had its inception in the early expeditions of Lewis and Clark and its culmination in the completion of the transcontinental railroad.

Uninterested in any notion apart from land as capital, most

homesteaders seemed oblivious to the fact that much of the region into which they were moving was characterized by an aridity of near-desert proportions. Though some who had explored the Plains before these mass migrations warned of exceeding limitations in their use, settlers chose to ignore what seemed to be only the pessimistic misgivings of naysayers. These men, as Worster illustrates, were seen as mocking the very providence of God,

> as enemies by all who identified freedom and democracy with national increase. Charles Dana Wilber, a town builder in Nebraska, felt compelled to answer them by an appeal to the Creator: it has never been God's intention, he announced, that any part of the earth be "perpetual desert." Wherever man "has been aggressive," he has made the land suitable for farming. . . . Rain would follow the plow, Wilber predicted; that was the way the Creator expected men to think. Turn the grasses under and the skies would fill with clouds.[20]

So turn the grasses under they did, and immoderately so. Not only was the number of people inhabiting these relatively small tracts of land disproportionate to the land's very modest carrying capacity, but the introduction of industrial-style agriculture began to place harsh demands on an already fragile ecological habitat. In contrast to the subsistence approach to agriculture, in which a small farm featured a variety of crops and livestock—a self-contained economic community—a rising breed of agricultural entrepreneurs began to realize that potentially huge profits lay in efficient production of an exclusive commodity on a grand scale. To this end investors began buying up larger tracts of land and sowing the fields in monocultures, massive single plantings of one grain, usually wheat. By the turn of the century the economy of the Central Plains depended solely on the sale of grain to brokers in distant cities like Chicago, men who rarely, if ever, saw the goods themselves, let alone the land on which they were produced.[21] But perhaps the most disturbing aspect of this industrial model of agriculture was yet another obstacle preventing the newly arrived immigrants from perceiving the morally compelling face of their surroundings: absentee ownership. Henry Ford's new technology had made it possible to work the soil without having to live on it. The machine now allowed for a strictly exploitative association with the land. A farmer did not have to live where he planted; he did not have to know his place. He only had to be there to sow the seed and reap the harvest (or hire others to do it for him) when it came time to collect on his investment.

After realizing immense profits in the sale of wheat during the First World War, farmers in the southern Plains states became all the more convinced of the wisdom of the industrial model of agriculture. Local newspapers began to hail the dawn of a new era and a future that was sure to see the establishment of a vital new urban center in the American heartland, a city whose culture would rival that of New York, or even Paris. This was indeed the Promised Land, where a little hard work with the right kinds of tools, and a good dose of shrewd business acumen, could transform a common man into a western wheat mogul. Now he, too, could provide his family with all the luxuries enjoyed by the aristocratic industrialists of the northeast. Gone were the days when the farmer was expected to live a life marked by frugality and thrift; the Plains, it seemed, were just as well suited to a capitalistic and consumptive lifestyle as any other region of the country, so let the standard of living be raised. Such were the glad tidings whispered by the amber waves of grain that now stretched in all directions toward the horizon.

But the revelry lasted only as long as the fields were sodden and the Chicago Board of Trade was singing a happy tune. A little over a decade later, in the 1930s, after the soil had been subjected to years of severe mechanical traction and relentless nutrient depletion, the rains no longer followed the plow, and the dust began to blow. Locals remember it as a time when driving dirt was a way of life: it settled on their evening meals, in their kitchen cupboards, on their finest Sunday suits. With the lack of rain came intense heat and the inevitable pestilent grasshoppers descending on whatever crops were able to survive the severe aridity. Suddenly, the self-proclaimed Promised Land of the previous decade was experiencing the wrath of the Creator in biblical proportions, and young farmers began to wonder if perhaps the sins of the fathers were now being visited upon the next generation. Indeed they were. Past transgressions against the land—the removal of its indigenous, deep-rooted species and the introduction of new annual crops, as well as the technological intervention that the maintenance of these required—now left many to wander in a desert of dust and darkness, seeking light but never finding it. Though the Roosevelt Administration eventually offered relief in the form of government checks, little could be done to remedy the loss of nutrient-rich topsoil that had been millennia in the making. The face of the Central Plains was carried by westerly winds to places as distant as Baltimore and Washington, D.C., and finally into the Atlantic Ocean, where it found its most unlikely resting place.

Through all this, some families chose to stay on their Oklahoma and Kansas farms, hoping to weather the storms (which finally did break in 1941). But most who came empty-handed to this region left with little more packed away in their jalopies, seeking new places, new fortunes, farther west. The mass of cultivators that Thomas Jefferson had extolled a century earlier as the American ideal, a breed with the sacred fire of morality burning deeply in their breasts, had become once again what they in fact had always been: mass migrators, transients, tragically incapable of discerning the face of their biotic communities, unable to find a home, but always seeking.[22]

This sense of homelessness did not subside after the turmoil of the dirty thirties. On the contrary, in the years following World War II, there was a mass exodus from the rural landscape to a less glorified type of Eden, the industrial centers of the nation, places where the face of the land was much more difficult to discern. But this transition was not entirely obvious to the masses, distracted as they were by the victory overseas and the prospect of a new day dawning. The myth of the family farmer remained an ever-present feature in the national psyche, in part as a result of the works of regionalist artists like Thomas Hart Benton and Grant Wood, who memorialized rural life in countless murals and paintings during and after the Depression. Thus, while the American people lived complacently with the notion that just outside their growing suburbs the traditional bucolic life of the yeoman farmer was still alive and well—was indeed the very backbone of this great nation—the truth was quite a different matter. The late 1940s, in fact, marked a watershed in American agricultural history. By this time the ideal was no longer the Jeffersonian husbandman, but the model of capitalist efficiency proposed by Adam Smith. Agriculture had become big business.

It did not take long for the effects of the industrial model of agriculture to be felt on the landscape itself. Had there ever been a pervasive tradition of the faithful farmer tilling and keeping his modest fields, it was certainly on the wane by mid-century. By now farming could best be described by a metaphor that had always lingered just below the surface of the American psyche, but one that had recently been a fixture in the national imagination: it was an act of war. The industrial agriculturist now began to employ the very armaments of military conquest in his or her campaign against the elements, and first among these was the prodigious use of chemical weaponry.[23]

This was hardly a coincidence. Having realized huge profits during the war effort, chemical manufacturers now needed a new and equally colossal market if the economic prosperity they had been enjoying was to continue. The battle against nature seemed to be just the ticket. And the farmers who did manage to remain on the land were certainly in need of a fix: their soils were no longer as productive as they used to be. Faced with decreasing ecological capital in their fields (that is, organic nutrients lost through years of erosion), they could now obtain credit in the form of inorganic fertilizers, herbicides, and pesticides. It was a kind of loan to make up for what had been squandered in years past. Replenishing the earth's nutrients by natural means would take decades, if not longer, and time was money; chemicals offered the very attractive means to maintain an efficient and productive operation. "Just a little something to keep you going," the industry said, and it was not long before both the land and the farmers—not to mention the American people—were addicted.

On the face of it, the plan seemed to work; after the chemical industry began expanding into the agriculture market, crop yields increased dramatically. Since the 1950s, Americans have lived in the midst of unprecedented food surpluses and have been graced with correspondingly low prices.[24] Today's supermarkets are indeed the grandest testimony to the so-called green revolution; rarely are shelves empty or understocked. For those of us born since mid-century, the hunger problem that accompanies so many forms of poverty in the United States, and especially in the two-thirds world, has never been a matter of a shortage of food but of its inequitable distribution. Our grain harvests are so bountiful that we are now compelled to use a portion of it to make ethanol, a fuel additive for our gas-guzzling vehicles. A growing number of homes in the Midwest are now burning dried corn to heat their houses; at approximately $2.00 a bushel, it is a very cheap alternative to natural gas. The chemical industry, of course, has not failed to celebrate this resounding success, assuring the public that they only want to keep us on the right track. But what they have too often failed to mention is the proportion to which their products have also wasted the face of the national landscape, destroying rural communities and debilitating human bodies along the way.

The American public first became aware of the potential threats of agricultural chemicals with the publication of Rachel Carson's now classic text, *Silent Spring.* An ecological prophet in her own right, Carson was concerned to expose, among other environmental hazards, the dangers of the widely touted pesticide DDT and its tendency to become concentrated in mammalian tissues as it works its way up the food chain (a phenomenon called bioconcentrating).[25] Though DDT appeared to work wonders on the production-oriented farms of the sixties, eradicating predators with admirable efficiency, its long-term consequences soon became a problem that could not be ignored or easily dismissed. Gradually, farmers began to notice deleterious effects on many beneficial species in the agricultural ecology, like the raptors, whose populations began to decline precipitously. (Not least of these was the bald eagle, a symbol of American strength and prosperity.) Finally, after much protest, DDT was banned for use as a pesticide in the United States (though it is still commonly used in many developing countries today).

For a while after these measures were taken, Americans seemed to be persuaded that the chemical companies had the situation well under control, that they would not deliberately market a product that could be harmful to public health. Nor would the Washington watchdog for ecological impropriety, the newly established Environmental Protection Agency (EPA), allow such practices to continue. But soon there was renewed cause for concern. In the early 1980s, routine tests of aquifers, underground wells, and natural water sources in rural districts around the Midwest revealed alarmingly high levels of inorganic contaminants—namely, fertilizers, pesticides, and herbicides. A number of investigations conducted during this time also found a very convincing correlation between the use of farm chemicals and elevated cancer rates in rural areas. As Osha Gray Davidson reported in *Broken Heartland*, an exposé of the American farm crisis, "one 1983 study determined that residents of Iowa counties in which large quantities of pesticides were used were 60% more likely to die of leukemia[, . . . and] farmers who use pesticides are more apt to develop Hodgkin's disease, non-Hodgkin's lymphoma, and cancer of the skin, lip, brain, stomach, and prostate."[26]

To the credit of the chemical manufacturers, though, measures were taken during the 1990s to curtail the amount of inorganic materials that were being used so profusely on the nation's cropland. These efforts would not, however, threaten the profit margins that these companies had come to depend on. In fact, the wave of environmental alarm and protest in the 1980s actually may have worked in the industry's favor; their response was to introduce new products that, apart from their advantages in the field, now also threaten to keep farmers forever under their rigid control. Instead of continued reliance on topical applications of herbicides, insecticides, and fungicides, these companies have turned to genetic engineering to solve the problem of environmental contamination, exploring the molecular structures of the crops themselves and devising novel ways to "improve" them. The result has been the modification of nearly every basic staple of the American diet, and this has raised a host of ethical questions that are just now beginning to be addressed.

A brief overview of some of the techniques involved in fashioning genetically modified organisms (GMOs) will help explain why so many today are worried about the future ramifications of these products throughout the world.[27] It will also serve to accentuate, even epitomize, the fundamental thesis of this chapter: that a mythology of conquest has so pervaded the Euro-American psyche that little in terms of a perceived moral responsibility toward one's place can curb its mastering or manipulation for personal gain.

The New Green Revolution

One of the most common practices for controlling weeds in agricultural fields has long been the repeated tillage of the soil, striking at the root of unwanted plants while maintaining the integrity of the desired crop. But as nearly a century of erosion has taught us, especially in the Great Plains, loosening the soil too regularly can produce disastrous results. Because of this, a technique known as "no-till agriculture" was developed in the 1970s that limited mechanical traction in the fields, thereby curtailing the amount of loose soil lost to wind and rain. But, by its very nature, no-till agriculture could not solve the perennial problem of weeds. Topical applications of herbicides could not be considered because they would have the counter-productive effect of eliminating the crop as well. It seemed, then, that the gains of no-till agriculture—reduced soil erosion—were entirely offset by its losses—an increase in noxious weeds.

In response to this dilemma, a number of agri-chemical manufacturers began venturing into the molecular structure of the crops themselves, modifying them by inserting into the genome of the corn or soybean plant, among others, a gene that renders the host immune to the lethal effects of a particular chemical herbicide. With this alteration the problem of topical applications of weed-killing chemicals is solved; spraying only affects those plants that do not contain the special gene. Not surprisingly, these custom herbicides are nearly always produced by the same company that creates the genetically modified seed.[28] They are sold as a set. Monsanto Company, for example, has created what it calls Roundup Ready crops that can withstand several topical applications of their very effective herbicide, Roundup. While unwanted weedy species are eliminated in a matter of days, the plants containing the introduced "protector gene" are left to flourish, albeit in a relatively sterile (in terms of biodiversity) ecological environment.

This new technique is not without its problems, not least of which is the potential for farmers, who want to be as efficient in their weed killing as possible, to be very liberal in their applications of Roundup. Though the manufacturer avows that the inert and active elements in the herbicide have no deleterious effects on the very fragile microflora of the soil or on human health, other researchers are dubious of the claim.[29] Also, in recent years extension agents across the country have been receiving more and more complaints from their constituents about "pesticide drift." When wind carries the chemical into adjacent fields, it inevitably kills whatever herbaceous vegetation it settles on; if the affected farmer is not using Roundup Ready crops, he or she stands to lose a portion of his or her investment.[30]

Thus, the pressure is on for more and more farmers to use this product, if for no other reason than as a preventative measure against foreign pesticide invasion. While this works to the advantage of Monsanto, it certainly limits the choices that a farmer can make when deciding what crops to plant and where to acquire the seed.

Genetic engineering has also been a tool for fighting the persistent problem of unwanted pests. Again, concerns over the effects of repeated topical applications of pesticides have turned the geneticists' focus to the plants themselves. This time, however, the solution has come from an unlikely (and none too enthusiastic) source: the organic gardener. For years, those committed to the ideal of chemical-free agriculture have used the bacterium *Bacillus thuringiensis* (*Bt*) as part of an integrated pest management approach to contending with destructive leaf-eating coleoptera and lepidoptera larvae. Organic growers apply *Bt* periodically to plants in powder or liquid form and when the unwanted worm ingests it, the bacteria work in the host's intestinal tract to starve the creature to death. On a small scale, the procedure is very effective, and one that prevents the unsightly corn-borer, for instance, or the tomato hornworm from destroying an entire kitchen garden. But what happens when *Bacillus thuringiensis* is used on a large scale? If the seed manufactures continue to market their technology at the current pace, it may not be long before we find out.

Geneticists have now developed the means of introducing *Bt* into the genes (and thus into the individual cells) of a number of common crops. Monsanto Company, once again, has been granted patents on *Bt* gene technology for use in its Bollgard (cotton), YieldGard (corn), and New Leaf (potato) products, and, as Marc Lappé and Britt Bailey report, their products have made steady inroads into the U.S. market. "In 1997, [Yieldgard comprised] 6 million of the total 80 million acres of corn,"[31] and that number has only increased in the years that have followed. But has this resulted in a lot of dead larvae, pests we no longer have to deal with? Not necessarily, for as any first-year ecologist knows, every species contains varietal mutants whose genetic peculiarities render them immune to toxins that would normally kill others in the group. They are black sheep of sorts but nonetheless vital to the process of natural selection, for in times of great duress, the last will often become the first. So it is with the lepidoptera and coleoptera larvae; while 99.9 percent of these creatures will be mortally affected by *Bt*, as many as 0.1 percent will go on living and reproducing as if nothing ever happened. And the more its less-adapted brothers and sisters die out, the more the black sheep's own toxoid-resistant genes will flourish in its environment, especially with acre upon acre of cropland to feed its voracious offspring. The eventual result could be a super-strain of pests against which the now highly effective *Bt* technology will be all but worthless. Organic gardeners will have then lost one of the few worthwhile defenses against unwanted predators in their gardens.

For all its technological sophistication, Monsanto has proposed a rather low-tech solution to the problem: farmers, they say, should plant a portion of their acreage in non-modified strains of the crop so that nonresistant larval species will still have a place to eat and eventually breed, thus keeping their toxoid-susceptible genes in the mix a little while longer. But this recommendation only raises red flags among those familiar with the self-serving inclinations of human beings. Without strict oversight, it simply establishes the conditions for an inevitable "tragedy of the commons." When left to make a moral decision calculated to serve the common good, men and women will more times than not opt to allow their neighbors to do the right thing while they continue on with business as usual. Expecting farmers to sacrifice sometimes as much as 20 percent of their fields and profits in order to prevent a potential environmental hazard reflects a very naive view of human nature, and one diametrically opposed to the fundamental tenets of free-market capitalism. Competition is the name of the game, not cooperation. *Bt* technology, then, appears to be an ecological disaster waiting to happen.

But by far the most disturbing trend among gene giants like Monsanto, DuPont/Pioneer, Novartis, and Dow—four companies that now control a major portion of the North American corn, soybean, and cotton market—is the development of what has been referred to as Terminator or Traitor technologies. Despite widespread protest in the United States and especially in Europe, these corporations have continued to move ahead with their plans to patent and market seeds that contain in their genetic structure "suicide genes," which render the seed sterile or at least unviable until the introduced gene is overridden by some form of chemical intervention. In other words, seeds are now being developed that will not germinate unless the consumer purchases and applies the necessary catalyst, a chemical "trigger." Furthermore, these corporations have tried to ensure that illegal seed saving on the part of those looking to cut costs does not go unpunished: Monsanto has made it clear that they will aggressively pursue the matter in court. Industry spokespersons claim that this is only good business: no one should be able to utilize a product to his or her advantage without compensating the owner of the patent. And they are certainly serious about repercussions.

In April 2001, a Canadian court ordered Percy Schmeiser, a third-generation Saskatchewan farmer, to pay Monsanto close to $85,000 for unauthorized use of their rapeseed (used to make canola oil), despite the fact that the presence of the GMO in his fields was the result of fertilization by pollen drift from a neighbor's GM crop. Thus, inadvertent pollination by patented plants is a legal liability that many farmers cannot avoid, apart from giving in, signing a licensing agreement, and planting the GMO itself. "It's like saying that Monsanto's technology is spreading a sexually transmitted disease," writes Hope Shand of Rural Advancement Foundation International (now the ETC group), "but everyone else has to wear a condom."[32]

And with this, it seems, the centuries-long desire of many in the West to subdue and have dominion over nature has reached its culmination.

So what has happened to the Garden, Eden, the holy grail of America's salvation and redemption? It has been objectified, commodified, advertised, and sold on the open market, to such an extent that in 2006, at this writing, a major portion of the world's food supply is legally manipulated and controlled by a handful of very powerful and very wealthy corporations. While they justify the genetic modification of crops with the apparently altruistic desire to feed hungry mouths in an increasingly overpopulated world, it is obvious to most that the ulterior motive lies in the huge profits that this endeavor will secure, not to mention the social and political control that comes with it.

But why should we be surprised at this? One of the fundamental tenets of the economic philosophy that we hold so dear is that human appetites are downright insatiable, that people will never be satisfied with enough. Augustine called it concupiscence. But capitalism has been able to flourish in this country and around the world because of the other side of our double-faced mythology. The narrative that has guided us from the beginning affirms for us all that Eden is here for our taking, that God's will demands of us an attitude of conquest, of production, of improvement, of subjugation and domination. In the end, with the Creator's blessing, we will prevail in the creation of a new world that is pleasing to God, a step up from the "satanic realm" into which our ancestors came so many years ago.

It is a tragedy indeed that our forebears did not listen to the voices of the original inhabitants of this land, men and women whose stories and rituals affirmed in no uncertain terms that the spirits of this place were, in contrast to the Judeo-Christian God, exceedingly pleased with the way it was. Improvements paled in importance to simple care of the land. Humans, in most Native worldviews, were here by invitation and grace, not by divine right, and their daily activities needed perpetually to reflect this awareness. Their "gods" were not distant but right here, watching, taking notice. Though Euro-Americans claimed also to believe in an immanent God, they tended instead to put their real money on divine transcendence, for they knew that if they were created in the image of such a deity, they, too, could lord it over the world in which they were placed. And lord it over they did, from the forced evacuations of Indians from their native places, to the repeated subjugation of the Great Plains ecosystem, all the way to the genetic "improvement" of their food crops (two in particular, corn and potatoes, being gifts from the Indians).

What, then, is to be said for the Judeo-Christian tradition? It is not difficult to see how, given the excesses of the past, many these days are more than willing to be done with it completely. But hope remains, I believe, in the most familiar narratives of the tradition and our faithful attempts to hear these anew in this place, informed by the myths that have preceded us here. It is to this task that we shall now turn.

4

Hearing Our Story
Again in This Place

Why Not Stewardship?

In the previous chapter we saw how the mythology of the Judeo-Christian tradition inspired an attitude of conquest among many who settled this land and how it has had its tragic effect on nearly every ecosystem on our continent, especially since the advent of so many technological innovations in the American agriculture industry. The church, it seems, has been powerless to stem the tide of this trend, primarily because it lacks the mythological and ritualistic means to impress upon its faithful the notion that their moral community extends well beyond its traditionally accepted bounds. At this point, however, some may be wondering why we have not dealt with a response to this predicament that has been a central tenet of the evangelical movement for decades. Why have I not yet said anything about "stewardship"?

The reason is twofold. First, what I will be proposing in this and subsequent chapters is a kind of stewardship model for the care of creation, or more specifically, for the care of one's place. However, and this is the second reason, I want to argue that the traditional understanding of Christian stewardship is in need of dramatic revision. In short, it is founded on the very anthropocentric Christian principles that are part of the problem needing to be addressed. Therefore, before I offer a revised understanding of this model, it will be helpful for us if we examine what theologians and others in the Christian community have proposed as the most suitable response to the ecological issues we face today.

Many Christians became aware of the need for a responsible relationship to the natural world in the late 1960s, primarily through the marketing of the "crying shame" commercial and through the growing interest in the environmental movement among the nation's young people. Earth Day 1970 may be seen as a kind of watershed in this respect; it inaugurated a new and widespread awareness of our need for change. For theologians, however, it was Lynn White's unsettling article that was the major catalyst for a new approach to thinking about creation and our place in it. Perhaps the most vigorous reaction to the essay came from evangelicals intent on exercising some form of damage control.[1] For them, the response involved a foray into some relatively uncharted theological territory. When considering the topic of "nature" or "the environment"—if they did so at all—most in this group tended to agree with the strongly anthropocentric and economically disposed perspective of one of their own, Thomas Sieger Derr:

> Man lives in the context of history and community and his decisions regarding nature must be responsible to that setting. He does not enjoy absolute right of disposition over natural resources, but is their steward, the caretaker of the Divine *owner*, using them and preserving their usefulness to future ages.[2]

"Nature," Derr goes on to argue, "is a complement to the primary drama of redemption which takes place in history."[3] Any concern for creation, from this point of view, must be ancillary to what is understood to be the fundamental theme of the

Bible: the providential acts of God toward God's chosen people. Consequently, all questions about ecology should be relegated to the theological file marked "stewardship," for, ultimately, these pertain simply to the task of putting one's house in order, taking account of how resources can be most efficiently used. This was seen as a responsibility not only to future generations (of humans) but to God, the rightful owner of the world.

Working under these assumptions, theologians and other scholars[4] responded to White, pointing out rightly that he had merely focused on those aspects of the biblical creation accounts that supported his thesis.[5] In their estimation, White had left too much unsaid. He had not considered the equally relevant portions of the narrative that admonish human beings to be God's representatives on earth. Yes, they conceded, the Creator does command humans to "subdue the earth and have dominion" (Gen. 1:28)—a verse to which White alludes but does not mention specifically—but this must be read and interpreted in light of the Yahwist account of creation: "The LORD God took the man and put him in the garden of Eden to till it and keep it" (Gen. 2:15). The use of the two Hebrew verbs, they argued, is particularly important here, for these give special insight into the true vocation of humans on this planet.

> Human responsibility is described by two verbs, *abad* and *shamar*. . . . The first of these . . . is often translated "till," but is sometimes translated "work" or "serve." And in fact, *abad* is the basic Hebrew word for "serve" or "be a slave to." The other word, *shamar*, is translated variously "keep," "watch," or "preserve." . . . Both verbs severely restrict the way the other two verbs—subdue and rule—are to be applied. Human ruling . . . should be exercised in such a way as to *serve* and *preserve* the beasts, the trees, the earth itself—all of which is being ruled.[6]

From this perspective, White's critique was based on an analysis of human history that has been informed by a fundamental misinterpretation of Scripture. Christianity is not the culprit here; rather, Christendom is. God calls human beings to be faithful stewards of creation, but throughout the centuries Christians have repeatedly forsaken this responsibility and occupied themselves with appeasing their own wanton appetites for wealth and substance. True believers, the evangelical apologists concluded, are preservers and sustainers.

But this response—which is still commonly maintained among many in the church today—misses White's point entirely, focusing as it does on a renewed sense of appropriate *action* in the world without seriously questioning our traditional notion of *being* in the world. On several occasions White even exposes the chink in his armor, practically begging for a constructive theological response: "What people do about their ecology," he writes, "depends on what they think about themselves in relation to things around them. Human ecology is deeply conditioned by beliefs about our nature and destiny—that is, by religion."[7]

What Christians have thought about themselves, and what evangelicals seem quite unwilling to relinquish or revise in any imaginative way, is that human beings are created exclusively "in the image of God," that they alone share "in great measure, God's transcendence of nature."[8] Indeed, the whole notion of stewardship rests squarely on this premise: the care of creation can only be entrusted to those who possess the ability to make important decisions objectively and rationally. But we have already seen where this can lead. Certainly the genetic engineer who has labored to increase grain production in America's heartland, or the chemist who has devised pesticides and fertilizers to ensure crop vitality, or the agri-business lobbyist who justifies the economic necessity of squeezing out the family farmer, has been heard to say that he is only being "a good steward of resources," that she is merely using her God-given abilities to make the best of a bad situation. And after all, what is more important than feeding all the hungry human mouths on this planet?

The stewardship approach, though widely affirmed in denominational statements throughout the Christian church, simply fails to meet the real ecological needs that we are facing today. In short, it is too open to abuse and manipulation. In addition to new ways of *acting* or *doing*, we need to set our sights on a transformed sense of *being* in our world and especially in our place. This will necessarily involve a much more constructive effort than merely reinterpreting Scripture within the parameters of an authoritative and monolithic teaching tradition. As we have already suggested, the real task before us is one of remythologizing, challenging the metaphors that we have so uncritically employed when discussing our identity and role on this planet and in our places. Only then will our sense of being in the world undergo transformation. And the place to begin, as Lynn White Jr. so helpfully indicated, is with our received understanding of what it means to be created in the image of God. So it is to the Judeo-Christian creation myth that we must turn once again in order to seek ways in which we can hear it anew in this place.

In the Image of Earth and of God

When we consider the manner in which Genesis 1—2:4a, the Priestly (P) narrative,[9] portrays God's creation of the cosmos, and the doctrines that subsequently grew out of this portrayal, it is not difficult to see how we in the Judeo-Christian tradition have come to regard ourselves as essentially removed or distinct from the rest of the natural world. The image we are given of the Creator informs and determines the image we have of ourselves, and this account presents a God who creates from a distance, an observer who *speaks* the cosmos into being and *sees* that it is good. Nowhere in this description are we given the impression that God "gets God's hands dirty" in the process, or that the quality and characteristics of creation are known through any tactile or first-hand experience. God does not taste or smell or feel the goodness of the earth in this story; rather, God contemplates it from afar, abstractly, as if surveying the blue-green jewel of a planet that Neil Armstrong first beheld from the moon in 1969.[10] In the Priestly account of creation, God is transcendent, wholly removed, and not to be confused in any way with the natural world.[11]

The Priestly narrative, however, is not the last word on God's creating activity. Another equally important tradition, the Yahwist's account, needs to be considered—and especially from this place where so many comparable cosmogonic myths have preceded us. Because of the peculiarities of God's early work in Eden, one can see why this story has become a favorite among gardeners. God, according to this tradition, is not a speaker of words as much as a planter of seeds. The Yahwist narrative (Gen. 2:4b—3:24) features a God who creates not from a distance but with God's own two hands. This is an account replete with sensuality. Here Yahweh walks through Eden in the cool of the day (Gen. 3:8), a garden that God has *planted* (Gen. 2:8). God calls out to the creatures there, encountering them face-to-face. But what is most distinctive about this narrative is the manner in which God creates Adam. One cannot help picturing some meticulous gardener, knees in the muck, hands full of rich, wet earth, who is undaunted by the mud on his face as he breathes the breath of life into the form beneath him: "then the LORD God formed man from the dust of the ground, and breathed into his nostrils the breath of life; and the man became a living being. And the LORD God planted a garden in Eden, in the east; and there he put the man whom he had formed" (Gen. 2:7-8).

The obvious pun in this account is lost in the English translation: "Adam" is a play on the Hebrew word *adamah*—earth, soil. We might suspect that upon hearing this story the early Hebrews understood very clearly who the original human being was and, consequently, who they were: Adam was an "earth child," brought into this world in the same manner as all the other creatures who roamed the earth (see Gen. 2:19). But what is perhaps most important in this narrative is the complete lack of any reference to humanity as "the image of God," let alone any affirmation of Adam's rational proclivities. On the contrary, a strong argument can be made that here we find humans created in "the image of the earth." Indeed, the only mention of any similarity with the Creator is in the *task* that Adam is later directed to perform: "The LORD God took the man and put him in the garden of Eden to till it and keep it" (Gen 2:15; see also Gen. 2:8). Just as the Creator nurtures and tends the garden that he has planted, so must Adam do the same; in this way, Adam "images" God. Thus we might say that the Yahwist narrative lends credence to the idea that human identity consists not in the ratiocentric *imago dei* (image of God) bestowed upon us by tradition, but in a much more ecocentric alternative: humans as *imago mundi et dei* (the image of earth and of God). Ontologically, we are grounded in the earth, with which we share our being. Ethically, our actions should reflect the work of the Creator—we are "imagers" of God.

It is at this point that we might pause to consider an interpretation of *imago dei* that has enjoyed particular favor among both Catholic and Protestant theologians since the middle of the twentieth century. As we have seen, the received notion of *imago dei* tended to place human beings outside or above the created order and has to some extent perpetuated the image of the ideal human as an autonomous individual who uses his or her cognitive abilities to discern God's will for creation. The assumption here is that there is some *substantive* similarity between the Creator and God's image on earth: as God is self-reflective, so are humans. The neoorthodox theologian Karl Barth took strong exception to this understanding of *imago dei*. For Barth, the suggestion of any essential affinity between a God who is Wholly Other and creation was, in his estimation, an affront to the Creator. In contrast to Augustine, Aquinas, and others who followed in their footsteps, Barth suggested that the divine nature is, at its most fundamental level, relational; Father, Son, and Holy Spirit exist in and enjoy an effusion of love among each other. In other words, God as Trinity is characterized by both an "I" who can issue a divine call and a "Thou" who can offer a divine response. This relationality, however, is not simply limited to the Godhead; it can also carry over into relationships with human beings who thereby share in this image of the Divine.

Thus the encounter that lies at the very core of God's being can take place on both an intra- and extra-Divine level.

> In God's own being and sphere there is a counterpart: a genuine but harmonious self-encounter and self-discovery; a free co-existence and co-operation; an open confrontation and reciprocity. Man is the repetition of this divine form of life; its copy and reflection. He is this first in the fact that he is the counterpart of God, the encounter and discovery in God Himself being copied and imitated in God's relation to man.[12]

For Barth, there is no "analogy of being"—that is, no shared essential nature—between God and human beings; rather, our claim to be God's image consists entirely in the fact that we have been graced with the distinction of being a Thou capable of encountering the divine I.

This singularity, however, is not simply a privilege—it has profound ethical implications. Though we share nothing ontologically with God, we are nevertheless obliged to act according to our received understanding of who God is. Like our Creator, we have been given the capacity to enter into relationships with others. We, too, are capable of being an I who may encounter a Thou in a spirit of reciprocity. Conversely, we are also likely to be called by others into meaningful and mutually affirming relationships. In this way we image God.

Barth establishes this assertion on what he calls the "analogy of relation." Just as the Godhead is fundamentally relational—Father, Son, and Holy Spirit—so must humans also see themselves. We reflect God's essential nature only when we acknowledge and affirm our most basic need to be related to others, to reach out beyond ourselves in a spirit of love. We are who we are by virtue of these encounters. Indeed, this is at the heart of the two great commandments that Jesus impressed upon all those seeking eternal life: "You shall love the Lord your God with all your heart, and with all your soul, and with all your strength, and with all your mind; and your neighbor as yourself" (Luke 10:27).

But herein lies the rub. Recall the lawyer's engaging response upon receiving these deceptively simple instructions from the Nazarene: "And who is my neighbor?" (10:29). For Barth, the answer was readily apparent: my neighbor is any Thou with whom I can enter into relationship—that is, any *human*. For all his innovation in reformulating this doctrine, Barth was not willing to move beyond the divine and human sphere when it came to meaningful relationships. But given the various ecological challenges of our present context, it should be evident that this perspective is just too short-sighted. It certainly does not take into account the very radical nature of Jesus' compelling reply to the lawyer's question: the parable of the Good Samaritan. This is less a story about ethics than about theological anthropology.

In first-century Palestine, the lines of the Jewish moral community were very clearly delineated; those who observed the laws of ritual purity and worshiped God in his proper place were not only deemed "good" by virtue of their deeds but in many respects recognized as truly human, chosen by God. By contrast, outsiders were not simply bad or immoral on account of their actions; in the eyes of many devout Jews, they were, by their very nature, unclean, even less than human. Jesus' parable, then, has implications that are easily lost on those of us who see in the Samaritan, an outsider to Jesus' culture, a *human* who demonstrates his love for another through his acts of kindness. In telling this story, Jesus was making a very deliberate attempt to shatter the conventional wisdom of his day and extend the bounds of the traditional moral community to include aspects of the world "out there," inhabited by creatures who were not widely regarded as fully human.

Given our current ecological concerns, we would do well not to overlook the centrality of the lawyer's earnest question: Who is my neighbor? To what Thou may I call out and receive an authentic and meaningful response, thus affirming my essential humanity as a relational being? Should humans alone populate my moral community, or should I rise to Jesus' challenge to break through old barriers and encounter this world anew? The land in which we Americans live has long produced tales in which humans were regarded merely as plain members of a Great Society, enjoying no special privilege or position of power. Ecologically, we know that we are indeed woven into an intricate web of life that, much to our dismay, regularly refuses to acknowledge our own self-styled importance. Theologically, however, we encounter obstacles to conceiving ourselves as having deep roots in this world, but only so long as we insist on our received understanding of what it means to be created in the image of God. Barth sends us part of the way down the road to recovery by insisting that the notion of *imago dei* be interpreted by an analogy of relation. I can agree with Barth that humans are called to be imagers of a relational God; my disagreement, however, is with his understanding of where and with whom we are to be doing our tilling and keeping.

If we can acknowledge our most basic ontological connection with the earth from which we and all other living creatures were formed—as the Yahwist suggests—we can then effectively begin to address the implications of the lawyer's question for our present context. My neighbor is any creature who was formed from the dust of the ground and with whom I therefore share my essential being. Ontologically, I am connected with the earth (*imago mundi*); ethically, I am called to image God by "serving" and "preserving" (*abad* and *shamar*) my neighbors (*imago dei*). The "care of souls," once so narrowly conceived, must now be expanded to include the "care of soils."

The point I am trying to make can perhaps best be illuminated by the reflections of the Roman Catholic geologist and theologian Pierre Teilhard de Chardin, a writer who has had a profound influence on many of today's leading proponents of creation spirituality. An interdisciplinarian who sought to reconcile the paradigm of Darwinian evolution with his faithful reading of the Scriptures, Teilhard proposed an elaborate cosmology in which the universe is conceived as creatively proceeding toward a divinely ordained telos, "the Omega point." In his mind, creation (as well as redemption) is not some once-for-all, static event but a perpetual process in which freedom and enlightenment are being attained. Nor is the cosmos merely the stage upon which the drama of human salvation is enacted; on the contrary, the universe itself reflects the spectacle of redemption in the very natural processes that can be observed with the aid of science and faith. "Teilhard's vision . . . is one in which the world is a vast whole making its way toward a supreme personality, a vision of the universe in the process of self-creation in which no breach [can] develop."[13] The entire universe is an evolution, or, as Teilhard preferred to call it, a "genesis."

Two aspects of Teilhard's thought are important for our purposes, for they offer insight into our ontological and ethical understanding of the *imago mundi et dei*. In the first instance, in opposition to the received dogma of his day, Teilhard established as a fundamental theological principle the idea that matter and spirit are not diametrically opposed aspects of our universe but rather two distinct features of a single substance or reality. Therefore, he critically challenged the false dichotomy of body and soul that has informed so much of orthodox theology. "The masters of the spiritual life," he writes, "incessantly repeat that God wants only souls. To give those words their true value, we must not forget that the human soul, however independently created our philosophy represents it as being, is inseparable, in its birth and in its growth, from the universe into which it is born."[14]

In this we can see Teilhard's firm insistence that, despite our conventional religious understanding of human origins, we in the modern era must accept what science tells us about ourselves: we were born from the earth—not just our flesh and bones, but our consciousness as well. The vast epic of evolution reflects a process of increasing individuation in which even the most rudimentary "juvenile matter" in the beginning contained a "quantum of consciousness" that gradually developed into the biosphere and eventually came to fruition in humanity itself.[15] In Teilhard's faithful estimation, the cosmos is essentially a living being, and its complete history is nothing less than an immense psychic exercise: the slow but progressive attainment of diffused consciousness. If this is the case, then humanity can very clearly be regarded as the image of the world, for we are "nothing but the point of emergence in nature, at which this deep cosmic evolution culminates and declares itself. . . . In the human spirit, as in a single irreplaceable fruit, the whole life of earth—that is to say, in brief, its whole cosmic value—is gathered and sublimated."[16]

Read in this light, the Yahwist narrative takes on a peculiarly universal nuance: Adam, as representative of the human race, is the living locus in creation where the cosmos becomes aware of itself. We might also add that, given Teilhard's understanding of genesis, spirit does not descend into the material world from on high for the purpose of supernatural animation. Rather, "the breath of God" (Hebrew: *ruah*; Greek: *pneuma*), so often understood as coming from without, in fact comes from within the evolving form of Adam himself/herself. Though he does not express the sentiment literally, Teilhard seems nevertheless to affirm the notion that humans, as creatures ontologically grounded in the earth, are in every sense the *imago mundi*.

But how is the *imago mundi* simultaneously the *imago dei*? Here, again, Teilhard is helpful, focusing as he does on the activity of humans in the world as they image the divine creative process. In his book *The Divine Milieu* Teilhard recognizes the tension that characterizes Christian existence, the question of whether one should distance oneself from the world or actively participate in it, shun community or seek it out. In his mystical vision he proposes a middle way, reconciling love for life with love for God, attachment with detachment. In order to subvert the traditional body/soul dualism while also affirming the wealth and diversity of human vocations (that is, the actual work of our hands), he employs a simple syllogism: all souls exist for God, and all material reality exists for our souls; therefore, the material world exists through our souls for God. The advantage of this assertion lies in the recognition that the human soul is inseparable from the matrix in which it is borne. The world that nourishes our flesh also enriches our spirit. In a very real way, one's soul is continually created by one's participation in the world process.

But this is not simply an individual endeavor whose end is shallow egoism. On the contrary, because of the interdependence of matter, soul, and the presence of God, which pervades all reality, the human being, through work, contributes in a small but significant way in the building of "the fullness of God" (Eph. 3:19; Col. 2:9) toward which all of creation is proceeding. If this is the case, then we must never be overly preoccupied with our individual activity. We must instead always maintain some sense of detachment so that our vocations never become a kind of *individual genesis*, and thus ends in themselves (a point to which we shall return shortly). As the Creator works continually through the universe (which, as Sallie McFague has suggested, may be regarded metaphorically as God's body[17]), toward the consummation of history *and* creation, so must humans in their work endeavor to image the redemptive activity of God. Humans are the *imago mundi et dei*. Ontologically, we are grounded in the earth; ethically, we are called to "image" God in our various vocations.

Despite Teilhard's rather attractive reflections, we cannot rely too heavily on his thought as we attempt to seek out neglected ecological nuances in our received creation mythology, and this for two reasons. In the first place, as we mentioned in chapter 1, Teilhard's concerns are so cosmological in scope that the particulars of human responsibility and commitment to a specific place tend to get lost in the enormity of his project. Wendell Berry's critique of global thinking applies well to Teilhard's meditations: "If you want to *see* where you are, you will have to get out of your spaceship . . . and walk over the ground." Though Teilhard posits a personalistic universe[18] (which does lend itself to the possibility of attributing moral value to the natural world), it is a *universe* all the same, and thus too vast and imposing to be considered personal on the basis of human experience.

Second, it is indeed ironic that Teilhard's greatest asset as a human being—his overwhelming optimism—may have in fact been his greatest liability as a scientist and theologian, and this is perhaps the most compelling reason for us to hold his physico-spiritual reflections at bay. His assumptions about the mechanism of evolution and the apparent direction of the process itself have now been so critically examined and challenged by evolutionary biologists as to be untenable for our present purposes. According to Stephen Jay Gould, for example, we can no longer naively presume that "progress defines the history of life or even exists as a general trend at all,"[19] or that humanity occupies some predetermined teleological prominence in the incredible matrix of life itself. Teilhard's faith may have affirmed this as a verity, but the most recent evidence does not support such a claim. In addition to this, it is certainly not in our best theological interest to follow Teilhard's lead in overlooking, or downplaying, the detrimental effects of sin and evil in the world. As we have noted, his was a vision of the universe caught up in the divinely directed process of self-creation, and, as such, it was a venture "in which no breach could develop." But, again, the evidence does not seem to be in his favor; we know all too well that breaches *do* develop, in both the cosmos and our native places.

Despite these objections, however, Teilhard de Chardin must be recognized as one who offers a helping hand as we continue on our way toward a renewed vision of our place in creation. His thought illumines an aspect of the Genesis narrative that has too often been overlooked or conveniently ignored: the idea that humans emerged from the earth and that this place of origin is fundamentally important in shaping our sense of identity. Far from being souls entombed in burdensome bodies, we are, like Adam, imagers of God, *imago dei*, when we recognize the interdependent connection between matter and spirit, God's work and our work, humanity and creation. That this relationship is affirmed throughout Scripture is a subject to which we will soon return, but only after we have considered an aspect of the human and cosmological condition that cannot be responsibly overlooked: the reality of sin in the world.

The Reality of Sin

Let us return now to our own emergence myth, the Yahwist account of creation. As the *imago mundi et dei*, Adam is characterized by the ability to enter into mutual relations with God, with the various nonhuman inhabitants of the earth, and with other humans. The original man and woman possess the capacity for empathy, for discerning the morally compelling faces of those in their midst. This is implicit in the fact that the Creator gives his imagers the distinguished responsibility of caring for their place, along with ample freedom to experience and explore their new domain. However, Yahweh also establishes an important prohibition: "And the LORD God commanded the man, saying, 'You may freely eat of every tree of the garden; but of the tree of the knowledge of good and evil you shall not eat, for in the day that you eat of it you shall die'" (Gen. 2:16-17).

Adam has enough at his disposal to serve the needs of his sustenance and comfort, and his vocation is such that he must till and keep these in order to continue in this ideal state. But, ironically, the very capacity that Augustine and Aquinas so enthusiastically proffer as humanity's most essential characteristic is in this account what most threatens, and eventually destroys, the original *shalom* of creation. Adam must not eat of the tree of the *knowledge* of good and evil, for it is by this act—the acquisition of intellectual discernment, a precursor to instrumental reason—that a fatal breach develops in the evolving consciousness of the cosmos. The *imago mundi et dei* forsakes his true identity and calling. The world is rent asunder, subjects are removed from objects, persons are differentiated from persons, souls from bodies, humans from the earth and from God, and always by means of some qualitative distinction: good versus evil. This much is attested in the narrative that ensues after the primal couple commit their transgression against God's command: alienated from himself, Adam is ashamed of his nakedness; enmity is placed between the serpent and Eve (or, more generally, between nonhuman and human creation); pain is visited upon the woman in the natural act of childbirth, and man is estranged from the earth in his labor (Gen. 3:8-19). Sin— separation, a denial of our essential relatedness—creeps into creation itself.

And so we have the story that has shaped the values of much of the Western world: men and women perennially plagued by a sense of disaffection, of rejection and guilt, because of a disruption in the integrity of the *imago mundi et dei*. And this breach of consciousness is not simply an existential affair; on the contrary, it is a brokenness that is experienced throughout the whole of creation. The earth from which Adam was formed falls along with him. Sin, therefore, is an ecological condition, affecting both the human and the nonhuman world. We have long been told that Adam's transgression in the Garden was simply an act of disobedience in opposition to Yahweh's prohibition and that our fallen nature can be attributed directly to this breach of contract. Adam breaks God's law and is justifiably punished. But focusing exclusively on this interpretation leaves too much unsaid; it overlooks the fact that Adam's real sin lies in his refusal to acknowledge his responsibility as an imager of God, a tiller and keeper of his place where his various relationships—with God, with Eve, with the animals, with the Garden as a whole—help to form his very identity. Certainly he ignores Yahweh's prohibition, but his more contemptible offense is his insistence on asserting his autonomy over the earth from which he was formed, his desire to break away and substitute his own ego for his original, relational sense of self. He becomes an "I" who stands alone. The separation that ensues between person and place— as well as the internal psychic anxiety known to all humans—is his most enduring legacy.

Sin and separation extend well beyond the interpersonal sphere, and it is important that this aspect of the myth of the Fall not be overlooked, for it explains why humans historically have been so prone to exercise divinely ordained dominion as an aggressive domination over the created order, a perversion of the Creator's intent. The ecological result of Adam's sin is tragically evident in the story of his two sons, Cain and Abel. As a "*tiller* of the ground" (Gen. 4:2), Cain is charged not simply with a mundane task, but with a vocation reminiscent of God's command to Adam: he is to be a dresser and keeper of all, a caretaker. As an imager of God, Cain's obligations no doubt extend to the protection and custody of his younger brother, Abel, "a *keeper* of sheep" (Gen. 4:2). Cain is the first-born and vainly believes himself worthy of carrying out the responsibilities and receiving the just rewards that this status entails. We can therefore sympathize with his bitterness and sense of rejection when events fail to follow the presumed logic of primogeniture (a recurring theme throughout the Hebrew scriptures).

> In the course of time Cain brought to the LORD an offering of the fruit of the ground, and Abel for his part brought of the firstlings of his flock, their fat portions. And the LORD had regard for Abel and his offering, but for Cain and his offering he had no regard. So Cain was very angry, and his countenance fell. (Gen. 4:3-5)

Cain makes his offering to Yahweh with an attitude of self-sufficiency; he believes he is valuable in and of himself, independent of any essential relations (to God, or to his brother, for instance). However, as soon as Cain grasps for his own autonomous existence—that is, as soon as he seeks favorable recognition from God—the singularity he so desires eludes him, and he is dejected and angry. His yearning for autonomous existence is foiled, as is inevitable with every human being. It is for this reason that Teilhard, in his cosmological analysis of the human condition, recommends as integral to human spirituality a kind of ultimate detachment—not from the world, as is often suggested by traditional statements of faith, but from one's ego.

As we participate in the genesis of the cosmos, we must constantly be aware of the temptation to allow our personal vocation to sink into a kind of shallow egoism. Teilhard suggests that as soon as *ego*-genesis takes the place of *eco*-genesis, becoming an end in itself—as it does in the case of Cain—a sense of isolation and rejection begins to set in. "Eternity is closed," as the Russian philosopher Nicholas Berdyaev observed, "and nothing but bad infinity is left."[20]

If allowed to fester, this estrangement from the rest of creation can have tragic consequences, as the ensuing biblical narrative indicates.

> Cain said to his brother Abel, "Let us go out to the field."
> And when they were in the field, Cain rose up against his brother Abel, and killed him. Then the LORD said to Cain, "Where is your brother Abel?" He said, "I do not know; am I my brother's keeper?" (Gen. 4:8-9)

It is fair to say that God's rejection of Cain's offering only accentuates an innate anxiety bequeathed him by his father, but Cain also possesses the means to overcome the condition. The Creator makes this very clear: "If you do well, will you not be accepted? And if you do not do well, sin is lurking at the door; its desire is for you, but you must master it" (Gen. 4:7). "Doing well" may be a bit misleading here, for it is what Cain must *not* do that will enable him to master the tragic lure of his anxiety: he must not allow the breach of consciousness growing inside him to manifest itself externally as sin, as ultimate separation from that with which he shares his ground of being. He must not permit ontological anxiety to actualize itself, to infect his doing, his vocation. Cain must refuse to succumb to the temptation to stand alone as an unqualified ego.

But succumb he does, asserting his independence and singularity in the most aggressive manner by murdering the one who shares his very blood, thereby disavowing his essential relatedness to any person or any being. The only way that Cain can ensure his autonomy and individual significance is to rise up against the other who threatens him. In allowing his psychic anxiety to manifest itself concretely as sin, Cain forsakes his *eco*-genetic vocation as a caretaker—"Am I my brother's *keeper?*" (Gen. 4:9; see Gen. 2:15)—and establishes as primary his own *ego*-genetic aspirations. But the separation that he willingly brings about has ramifications that extend well beyond the inter-human sphere, as God implies in his condemnation of Cain's act: "And the LORD said, 'What have you done? Listen; your brother's blood is crying out to me from the ground! And now you are cursed from the ground. . . . It will no longer yield to you its strength; you will be a fugitive and a wanderer on the earth'" (Gen. 4:10-12).

As *imago mundi et dei*, Cain's attempt to stand alone is not merely an existential phenomenon but in fact an "eco-stential" affair, as Scripture attests. The breach of consciousness destroys the integrity of the *imago mundi et dei*, seeping into the very soil that gives rise to the being of Cain himself. From thence forward, the eldest son is separated from his Creator, from his family, from himself, *and from the earth*. "Place," in the words of G. K. Chesterton, becomes "the wrong place."[21] Cain's self-assertion prevents him from knowing the language of the fields, from recognizing the morally compelling faces in his midst. The ground "no longer yields to him its strength," because in his attempt to establish his separation from it, he can no longer discern its wisdom. He is consigned to live forever east of Eden in the land of Nod, the land of wandering. And it is no coincidence that at this juncture Cain, a gardener and a gardener's son, forsakes his original vocation and builds a city (Gen. 4:17-22), a self-contained fortress where the *imago mundi et dei* can endeavor vainly to become *imago sui*, "image of my self," and where the natural world on the outside can be regarded erroneously as "other," as object and adversary.

And so we have one of the best-known stories in the Western world, retold and relived for countless generations. In allowing his psychic anxiety to manifest itself concretely as sin—that is, as separation—Cain is the symbolic representative of those throughout history who have denied their essential relatedness to God, to humanity, and to the earth, and whose aggression has led us tragically into our present century, as our contemporary social and ecological problems attest. Who among us today will dispute that we are still living "away from the presence of the LORD, . . . in the land of Nod, east of Eden" (Gen. 4:16)?

But, as is so often the case throughout Scripture, this state of affairs is only the penultimate word on the human condition, for the grace of God has from the beginning offered a hopeful admonition to all regarding sin: "you must master it." The breach of consciousness may be mended, the original *shalom* of the garden may be restored, the *imago mundi et dei* may once again know peace and repose. But the change will not come by "going home," west toward Eden—Americans have by now recognized the shallowness of this once-promising possibility. Rather, the time is ripe to heed the wisdom of simply staying put, of digging in and making peace with the earth, the ground of our being. And the time has come to hear once again a more hopeful story in this place, one of reconciliation with those who rise up to meet us where we are, be they human or nonhuman. The time has come to hear with new ears the messiah's story.

The Messiah's Story

As we have seen, a fundamental tenet of evangelical theology has been the notion that history is the arena in which the God of Israel most perfectly reveals God's mighty acts, where Yahweh enters into covenant after covenant with a wayward but nevertheless chosen race. Nature, by contrast, has been conceived merely as the stage upon which the work of redemption is enacted. Though this has been an inspirational theological theme for the past four hundred years, it has nevertheless been mired in what we have been alluding to as the original sin of humanity, that is, the tendency to abstract ourselves from the earth, from the place of which we are an integral part. I would suggest that although God's providential goodness in history is a prominent theme in both the Hebrew Bible and the New Testament, it is a misreading of Scripture to assume that it is the most important theme. Indeed, when interpreted in light of our proposed understanding of humanity as *imago mundi et dei*, Yahweh's mighty acts in time seem ultimately to be directed toward some eventual fulfillment in space. In other words, our remythologizing has now taken us to the point of establishing the idea that, contrary to the received dogma, *history* is in fact the vehicle or means by which *nature* is redeemed.

In his now classic text *The Land*, Walter Brueggemann suggests that throughout the Hebrew Bible, land—or what we have been referring to as "place"—is a fundamental theological category and crucial for the fulfillment of Yahweh's redemptive acts in history. According to Brueggemann, the story of the Hebrew people—from slavery to monarchy to exile to tenuous return— is the tale of a perpetual quest for a place to belong. Land, he suggests, is often used metaphorically in Scripture "to express the wholeness of joy and well-being characterized by social coherence and personal ease in prosperity, security, and freedom," but this should not obscure the importance of the idea's literal implications as "actual earthly turf where people can be safe and secure, where meaning and well-being are enjoyed without coercion."[22] The Hebrew scriptures continually move back and forth between literal and symbolic intent.[23]

To illustrate his point, Brueggemann first considers Yahweh's covenant with Abraham (Gen. 12:1ff)—"go . . . to the land that I will show you"—and suggests that with this story the book of Genesis embarks on a new history. Whereas the preceding narratives (Genesis 1–11) pertain to a people rooted in a place, who "presume upon the land and lose it,"[24] the story of Abraham and his descendants (Genesis 12–48) offers a kind of mirror-image of what has gone before. Here we have an account of a people who is without land but nevertheless continually on its way toward land, empowered by its anticipation of Yahweh's promise. It is this history that Americans feel perhaps most keenly, for like Abraham, "our lives are set between expulsion and anticipation, of losing and expecting, of being uprooted and rerooted, of being dislocated because of impertinence and being relocated in trust."[25] Yet in our tendency to overlook the details of our myths, we Americans have been most reluctant to grasp the fact that, as with the seed of Abraham, occupation of a Promised Land always comes with a divine charge to be responsible caretakers—tillers and keepers—to be so faithful in our vocation that our obedience to God's command, our imaging of God, becomes expressly manifest in our place.

This is an essential component of perhaps the most important covenant that Yahweh makes with his people, the presentation of the Torah at Mount Sinai. As Brueggemann suggests, though the teaching was first delivered to the Hebrews during their sojourn in the wilderness, at a time when they experienced landlessness in its most extreme form, "a case can be made that Torah becomes relevant in decisive ways for Israel only when it is landed, not in the yearnings of the fathers, not in the weariness of slavery, not in the precariousness of sojourn, but singularly in the land. Only in land is Israel primarily people of the Torah."[26] It is when God's chosen have reached their destination, have found their place, that they can truly demonstrate their faithfulness to the covenant at Sinai: refusing to covet and control what gives them their unique sense of identity and security; allowing not only for a human but for an agricultural sabbath (Leviticus 25); accepting the landless poor as brothers and sisters in God's covenant (Deut. 15:1-18; 22:1-4).

Though land presents the temptation and perpetual opportunity for the once-oppressed to become oppressors, to become coercive and manipulative in their dealings with "the other," the people possess the ability not to recapitulate the transgressions of their earliest ancestors. By remembering the precariousness of their own existence, recalling the wandering in the insecure space of the wilderness, and then acting responsibly and thankfully in accordance with the law, Israel may be deemed acceptable in God's sight. Once again, Cain's story is everybody's story, for in the Promised Land, the Torah evokes Yahweh's stern admonishment: "If you do well, will you not be accepted? And if you do not do well, sin is lurking at the door; its desire is for you, but you must master it." Doing well, for a people living in place, means affirming as individuals and as a community every nuance of humanity's original creation as *imago mundi et dei*. This is righteousness.

Though examples abound throughout the Hebrew scriptures of the necessary connection between humans and place, history and nature, we must here mention only one final instance of the implied *imago mundi et dei* metaphor. As is well known, the subsequent chronicles of the Hebrew people are marked by an uneasy tension, even during the prosperous years of the monarchy, which eventually disintegrates into the kind of division and animosity worthy of only the most self-absorbed descendants of Cain. The land divides, different theological traditions develop according to the collective memories of each kingdom, and a rivalry between sibling nations ensues until each has met its own final calamity. Yet, amid this dissension the still small voice of Yahweh continues to speak through some of the most unlikely messengers—the prophets, those persistent gadflies who buzzed around the ears of a complacent urban society, admonishing the people of God to remember their covenanted obligations to their creator, to each other, and to the land itself. Men like Amos, Hosea, and Jeremiah, among others, spoke of the insidious destruction of their homeland, for the blood of Abel, in their estimation, continued to infect the integrity of creation. All was broken, and all appeared to be lost.

But, again, judgment is always the penultimate word in Scripture, for redemption is primary in the Creator's heart. And the vision of renewal offered by Micah of Moresheth, a rural prophet who spoke to both Israel and Judah, reflects an often overlooked aspect of Yahweh's reconciliation with a wayward people. Micah foresees a day when a righteous king, a messiah, will, by his very presence in the land, remind the people of their original creation as *imago mundi et dei*. Sibling rivalry, division and strife, will cease, but more importantly, the well-being of the land it-self will be restored as Yahweh's people reaffirm their true identity and vocation as tillers and keepers.

> For out of Zion shall go forth instruction,
>   and the word of the LORD from Jerusalem.
> He shall judge between many peoples,
>   and shall arbitrate between strong nations far away;
> they shall beat their swords into plowshares,
>   and their spears into pruning hooks;
> nation shall not lift up sword against nation,
>   neither shall they learn war any more;
> but they shall all sit under their own vines and under
>   their own fig trees,
>   and no one shall make them afraid;
> for the mouth of the LORD of hosts has spoken.
>   (Micah 4:2-4)

It is important to note that this eschatological vision does not involve some final separation from the earth of which humans are a part, as many premillennial Christian sects would have us believe. Indeed, when considered in light of the theme that we have been exploring, such a suggestion would really amount to a kind of scriptural non sequitur. What does seem clear, however, is that the messiah referred to in this prophecy is conceived as an emancipatory and redemptive presence manifesting the law, and thus the will, of Yahweh peaceably in a particular place, suffusing the earth, not with the spilled blood of a slain brother, but with righteousness, well-being, *shalom*. When the messiah, or anointed one, is finally established in his kingdom, the sense of rejection and separation that characterizes so much of human existence will at last be dispelled. The fig, which in the narrative of the Fall is a symbol of shame and separation, will on this day be transformed into an emblem of peace and repose. In short, the breach of consciousness that has for millennia rent the soul of the *imago mundi et dei* will be mended. Or, as Micah tells us, "the former dominion shall come" (4:8); history *and* nature will be redeemed. No longer will the life of Adam and his wayward sons be the metaphor that best characterizes human existence, for on this day the messiah's story will be everybody's story.

The conventional understanding of Christian stewardship, dependent as it is on a traditional conception of humanity as separate from the earth and rationally and objectively able to discern God's will for the proper use of creation, is no longer sufficient for meeting the demands of our most pressing ecological problems. Indeed, some, like Lynn White Jr., have suggested that it is less a solution to the problem than its underlying cause. Modifying our actions merely to conform to the monolithic teaching tradition of the past simply offers too little too late; we need instead to reform our understanding of who we are and what is required of us. We are the *imago mundi et dei*. Formed from the dust of the ground, along with every other earthly creature, we can no longer deceive ourselves into believing, like Cain, that we can somehow stand alone, removed from the world. As Chief Seattle is reputed to have said, "what befalls the earth, befalls the children of the earth." And the reverse of this, as we have just seen, is also true. Our likeness to God lies not in some substantive essence, but in our capacity for entering into authentic reciprocal relationships—with God, with humans, *and with the nonhuman inhabitants of our place.* We are called to be like the Creator in our tilling and keeping, in the serving and preserving of our neighbors. Another way to say this: we are called to affirm that the care of souls, so long a central concern for the church, must necessarily entail the care of soils.

Thus we have the foundation for a thoroughgoing creation spirituality, and one that is not too far removed from models proposed by contemporary theologians whose inspiration lies in the physico-spiritual reflections of Teilhard de Chardin. But our most basic question still remains: Do we really want a *creation* spirituality? Should I be content in knowing that I am the image

of *the world* and of God? Given the scope of such a project—
the fact that the universe dreams me and that I must respond
accordingly—can I ever get a tangible sense that my vocation,
the relatively meager work of my hands, is actually bearing fruit
in some meaningful way? Furthermore, when we recognize the
pervasiveness of sin in our world and Yahweh's admonition that
"you must master it," is the cosmos really the best context for
me to go about this task? True, it is my *ultimate* context, but I am
more likely to feel a much stronger kinship and responsibility to
the myriad faces—human and nonhuman—who, by encountering me in my *place*, help to make me who I am.

To many, a large-scale spirituality is very attractive because it
appears to lack all the undesirable encumbrances and trappings
of what they regard as "religion." The problem with this, however, is that community—the place where one can cultivate an
abiding sense of the Eternal You through discipline and ritual—
becomes very ambiguous indeed. What is needed, then, is a way
to focus our attention, a way to bring creation spirituality down
to earth. What is needed is a theology of place.

5

A Theology of Place

Thinking Locally

As we move further into a new millennium, it is instructive to take note of two seemingly unrelated and opposing intellectual trends—one economic, the other theological. First, we have (if we are to believe the prognostications of its enthusiasts) a virtual panacea for solving the world's most pressing material problems: globalization. With the development of computer technology and other advances in communications, it is now possible to apply the tenets of laissez-faire economics on a worldwide scale, and all for the benefit of the common person—or so we are told. But as more than ten years of free trade across national borders has demonstrated, this paradigm dictates the parameters of nearly every other human concern as well—from education, to politics, to food, to social and ecological health—and its ripple effects are being felt most egregiously among the poor in the two-thirds world.

Since the 1995 passage of the Uruguay Round of General Agreements on Tariffs and Trade (GATT), nations across the globe have had to capitulate to a number of key concessions, lest they miss the boat entirely on the alleged rising tide of prosperity. Failure to do so would mean certain censure by the World

Trade Organization (WTO) and thus inevitable economic collapse. The basic formula for achieving global abundance is deceptively simple: participating countries must (1) remove all national trade tariffs; (2) abolish all rules hampering foreign investment; (3) eliminate price controls but impose wage limits; (4) convert self-sufficient, small-scale agriculture to corporate, export-oriented monocultures.[1]

The most evident result of these initiatives, however, has not been a more equitable distribution of wealth and resources among the poor but a widening disparity between the "haves" and the "have nots" on this planet. Equally alarming is the fact that there has also been an increasing homogenization of the world's diverse cultural traditions. To give just one unsettling example, it is estimated that the human race is now losing at least one indigenous language every two weeks, and this number is expected to increase in the years ahead. If our words, metaphors, and idiomatic expressions are part of the foundation on which our cultures are constructed, then corresponding lifeways are lost as well. If this trend continues, it is conceivable that within the next few decades a person will be able to travel from California to New York, across Western and Eastern Europe, and to the Far East, all the time eating in the same restaurants, encountering people wearing the same clothes and speaking the same language, and seeing farmers' fields planted in the same genetically modified crops. "Local flavor," in other words, is quickly on the wane.

Almost from the beginning of deliberations about the Uruguay Rounds of GATT and the North American Free Trade Agreement (NAFTA), there has been an informed and very vocal minority who have opposed the new global economy. They see it less as a solution to the world's most pressing problems than one of their chief causes. Not least of their concerns is the perceived threat to a host of democratically determined laws and health standards both in the United States and around the world. Regulations governing clean air, for example, or the right to earn a decent living wage can be easily trumped by the WTO as "non-tariff barriers" to free trade and therefore hindrances to the optimum efficiency of the global marketplace. There is also a great concern for the threat that new biotechnologies pose to the well-being and diversity of our planet's flora and fauna, not to mention the potential harm these could do to local cultures and traditions. But there is a way out of this predicament, opponents argue, and it involves becoming more consciously attuned to the needs, limitations, and strengths of one's particular community. "Thinking locally," they suggest, is the first and perhaps most important corrective to the runaway train of globalization.

Of particular interest for our purposes is the philosophical approach to local vitality known as bioregionalism, that is, a means of defining a geographical area of any country not according to the boundaries arbitrarily imposed by the county, state, or nation, but in terms of the ecological idiosyncrasies of the region. In many respects, the suggestion is that we return to an understanding of place that was common among the indigenous peoples of this continent well before Europeans arrived with their charts, maps, and four-square grids. A central feature of this eco-political outlook, as Kirkpatrick Sale has indicated, is a principal emphasis on the need

> to understand *place*, the immediate, specific place where we live. The kinds of soil and rocks under our feet; the source of the waters we drink; the meaning of the different kinds of winds; the common insects, birds, mammals, plants, and trees; the particular cycle of the seasons; the times to plant and harvest and forage—these are the things that are necessary to know.[2]

Sale also believes, along with Aldo Leopold, that humans cannot be abstracted from their local ecology, as if we somehow simply dwell *on* the land instead of *in* it. Rather, humans should be recognized collectively as comprising *one* of the fundamental communities of any bioregion. Our cultures—our stories, traditions, food, languages, and customs—have grown up out of the very soil of our "life-places" (to use bioregionalist Robert L. Thayer's term), and they have been shaped in large part as a response to our physical surroundings. The care of one's place, then, including a concern for its economic health, presents itself as a very viable alternative to globalization: it focuses less on the exploitation of resources than on their conservation; it is more interested in cooperation among community members than in competition; it chooses to emphasize the importance of preserving diversity and evading wholesale uniformity. This last point should not be overlooked. Whereas the tenets of globalization demand the establishment of monocultures across the world—the homogenization of nearly everything that comprises a community in place—bioregionalism maintains that the health of any life-place lies in its internal heterogeneity and particularity. Thus it rejects the newly emerging "McWorld-view" on every level and promotes the value of cultivating a very intimate familiarity with the sufficiently beguiling world that lies just outside our own back door.

In the last three decades a similar move toward affirming the importance of diversity and contextuality has also taken place in the area of theology, and this is the second intellectual trend that merits our consideration. Just as bioregionalists have opposed the move toward homogenization in the economic sphere, so have liberation theologians contested what they perceive to be a similar tendency in the history of European theology. As Enrique Dussell has suggested, the latter is a kind of false consciousness, a "theology of the center," whose "I" fashions itself primarily along Cartesian lines: "I think; therefore I am." The inevitable result of this, as we have already seen, is an undue emphasis on the importance of the rational subject and a complete reduction of all other entities in the world to the status of object. Thus the "I" of European theology, Dussell argues, is conceived almost necessarily as an "I conquer," or an "I against it," as attested by the lives and careers of the Spanish Conquistadors Hernan Cortes and Francisco Pizarro and so many others who have followed in their wake.[3]

Theology done from this vantage point—like economics con-

ceived along global lines, I would add—cannot help being oppressive in its very structure and effect. This is not the way the
poor of Latin America have interpreted their experience of the
God they meet in the gospel and in the faces of the others whom
they encounter in their hope for liberation. In light of this, as
Gustavo Gutiérrez has argued so persuasively, a new way of
doing theology is required to address the very concrete questions being asked in social locations where poverty and persecu-
tion are everyday realities. A theology that "thinks globally" and
"acts locally" tends simply to gloss over, if not exacerbate, the
diverse needs of men, women, and children living in these distinctive contexts throughout the world.

In response to their various experiences of economic and political oppression, Latin American liberationists have effectively
turned the tables on the received Enlightenment-style methodology of Western European theology. To consider their approach
is like taking a step into Jesus' kingdom of God, for what is con-
ventionally regarded as last here becomes first. It is spiritual reflection done from "the underside of history." One's primary
theological perspective, liberationists argue, must not simply rest
on the old Cartesian dictum, "I *think*; therefore I am"; rather,
it must be contextually focused: "I *am*; therefore I think." In
other words, one's theological starting point cannot be the false
consciousness of a self abstracted from a particular community.
We *are* by virtue of *where we are*, and our questions must reflect
this reality, lest they become irrelevant and, consequently, pliant
tools for spiritual despotism.

The place to begin is not with the individual self but with
"the other," my neighbor, the one whom I encounter in a particular social setting. In so doing, my questions will first be directed not to my own curiosities but to the needs of the one
who stands before me. This empathic approach, as Gutiérrez
has suggested, lies at the very heart of the gospel itself.

Love of one's neighbor is an essential component of
Christian existence. But as long as I define my neighbor
as the person next door, the one I meet on *my* way, the one

who comes to me for help, my world will remain the same. All spirit of individual "aid and assistance," all social reformism, is a "love" that stays on its front porch. . . . But if, on the contrary, I define my neighbor as the one whose way *I* take, the person afar off whom I approach, . . . then my world changes. This is what is happening with "the option for the poor," for in the gospel it is the poor person who is the neighbor par excellence.[4]

One can see the challenge this approach presents to the methodological assumptions of traditional theology. Whereas for the latter the fundamental starting point is the thinking subject, the person contemplating as nearly as possible something akin to Plato's forms—verities about God, Christ, humanity, and so forth, whose validity is in no way affected by the social context of the theologian—the primary point of departure for liberationists is "critical reflection on Christian praxis in light of the Word."[5] And this is not a static but an ongoing dialectical activity: what and whom we encounter in our day-to-day lives will perpetually affect and refine our reflection on the gospel and its relevance to our particular context. Juan Luis Segundo has referred to this as the "hermeneutical circle" where "each new reality obliges us to interpret the word of God afresh, to change reality accordingly, and then go back and reinterpret the word of God again, and so on."[6]

In light of this, we can see how theology becomes a "second act," entered into only after we have (1) recognized and critiqued the social structures responsible for the oppression of a particular community, (2) interpreted these in light of the liberating message of the gospel, and (3) taken into consideration the experience of our Christian practice in our particular context. Only then is the stage set for reflecting on the spiritual significance of our work and our encounters. As Gutiérrez has remarked, alluding to Hegel, "theology rises only at sundown."[7] It should only be done, I would add, with dirt on one's hands.

One aspect of liberation theology that will be helpful as we begin to consider thinking locally is the means by which the gospel is shared with others in a particular community. Certainly praxis and proclamation play an important role, but these are not entirely sufficient for the prodigious task of communicating the good news. This awareness has led women and men of diverse base ecclesial communities throughout Latin America to acknowledge the validity of various means for affirming in their places the liberating power of Christ. Indeed, the people in these local settings seem to take very seriously the old dictum "preach the gospel, and if necessary use words." In contrast to the logocentric European tradition, the emancipatory Word of God is conveyed effectively through dance, song, and the visual arts, all the time using local artifacts to express their experiences of liberation in light of the gospel message.

For example, in the collection of engaging prints published several years ago, *The Gospel in Art by the Peasants of Solentiname*, the story of Jesus' birth, life, death, and resurrection is depicted as taking place in the rain forests and verdant valleys of Nicaragua. Here Herod's soldiers, in the slaughter of the innocents, are dressed not in the imperial garb of first-century Palestine but in the khaki military uniforms of Somoza's death squads.[8] To the people of Solentiname who produced these paintings, no Western-style hermeneutical leap was necessary for imagining what Jesus' oppression at the hands of the Romans must have been like. They lived it daily. Likewise, stories, so notable in Native American traditions, are regarded as very effective means for expressing the unique theological insights of a victimized people living in place. Certainly the gospel message is essential to their lives of faith, but so are the tales of individual experiences—of memories, hopes, dreams, and disappointments—told by people of all ages in a receptive and supportive base ecclesial community. The ability to hear and reflect on these local stories from the underside of history is also central to the task of liberation theology. The narratives themselves help to convey so many subtle nuances of a people's unique liberating experience of God by utilizing words, illustrations, and expressions familiar to a particular social context.

It would seem then that liberation theology provides a very

helpful foundation on which we might begin to construct a tenable theology of place, one that seeks to engender a sense of emancipation and reconciliation among all members of a specific community. Theologians like Gustavo Gutiérrez, Juan Luis Segundo, Enrique Dussell, and others have very effectively exposed the shortcomings of a European theological tradition that thinks globally. A "one-size-fits-all theology," they suggest, serves only to discount the unique spiritual needs of a particular community, undermining an appreciation for its diversity and singularity. Traditional theologians, liberationists argue, need to take seriously the multifariousness of the world; in so doing, they will recognize the futility of their received methodology.

We are now seeing the economic effects of globalization in the two-thirds world: cultures are being destroyed, languages lost, biodiversity threatened, all in an effort to create a thoroughgoing McWorld-view. And this raises several questions that we in the first world would do well to consider: What, for example, is the connection between this relatively recent economic trend and European "theology as usual"? Has the latter served in any way as a tacit justification for the former? Are European theologians, as described by liberationists, the original global thinkers, the paradigmatic prototypes for economists who now envision a new world order? With regard to ecological theology, does the recent attempt by some to establish a single unifying creation narrative—a "universe story"—merely perpetuate the oppressive agenda that liberationists have critiqued so thoroughly? Will it liberate? If so, who will be its beneficiaries? Should we not be open to the possibility that in this we are dealing once again with yet another instance of top-down, one-size-fits-all theology?

I do not want to imply that liberation theology is not without its own shortcomings; on the contrary, it is questionable whether it is sufficient in itself to ground a truly liberating theology of place. It, too, suffers from a shortsightedness that suggests its break from Enlightenment-style thinking has not been as radical as we might think. Its critique of traditional European theology has been that it needs to be open to the voices crying out from the underside of history, and this is a very valid observation. Yet I would suggest that most liberationists also need to hear the more subtle laments arising from "the underside of the underside"—the nonhuman inhabitants who make up any biotic community.

As I mentioned briefly in chapter 1, theologies of liberation have for several decades been entirely too anthropocentric in their focus (with the notable exception of eco-feminism). When speaking of the oppressed or the poor, the emphasis has nearly always been on human subjects. My neighbor, as we saw in the Gutiérrez quote above, is nearly always "the [human] person afar off whom I approach." Rarely is it suggested that a social location, the point in history at which liberation occurs, is at once a biotic community, that it includes all creatures sharing a particular place. Indeed, when it comes to thinking about the nonhuman world, many liberationists seem to fall in line with Thomas Sieger Derr's position that "nature is a complement to the primary drama of redemption which takes place in history."[9] They have not, therefore, gone far enough in proclaiming the reality of God's love and preferential option for a much more radical underside of history, a base *ecological* community. Most have not acknowledged the fact that oppression, like the blood of Abel, does not simply pool around the bare soles of so many downtrodden men, women, and children. It seeps into the very earth itself, and from there it cries out.

Solidarity with the poor, then, means much more than engaging in liberative work among the forgotten human victims of unjust social structures. It means thinking in a new way about the lawyer's question to Jesus: Who is my neighbor? While European theologians certainly have much to learn from the liberationists of Latin America and other parts of the world, the latter might also gain new insights from both bioregionalists and Native American creation myths that recognize humans as merely plain members of a Great Society.

As I also mentioned in chapter 1, my own thinking on what a more holistic theology of liberation might look like grew out of my experience of living for several years in the Cumberland Mountains of eastern Tennessee. This part of the country, perhaps more than any other, needs desperately to hear the good news of God's preferential option for the poor: the men and women who live here, as well as the various other inhabitants of the bioregion, have for more than a century endured the devastating effects of big business bent on reaping quick and easy profits. First, the allure was timber, vast stands of old-growth oak, poplar, hickory, and pine growing on land whose owners could easily be hoodwinked into handing over the logging rights. With coal mining the story was pretty much the same. In all of this, locals were regarded as little more than pawns, there to be used when the conditions were favorable, or abused if they got in the way.

In the 1930s, for example, farmers along the Tennessee River were forced to sacrifice their homes to the newly established Tennessee Valley Authority, whose water works projects, officials assured the displaced, would only serve the greater good of the region. One of the key beneficiaries of this development was the Oak Ridge National Laboratories complex that offered low-wage jobs to a compliant and uneducated labor force and eventually produced the atomic bomb that destroyed Hiroshima in 1945. Today, the water and land surrounding this facility are among the most heavily polluted in the country, and community health is a critical problem that is not being adequately addressed.[10]

Living in Appalachia, one cannot help being aware of the effects of so many past injustices, whether it be the frequent flash floods that now result from hillsides devoid of timber, or human neighbors suffering from a host of environmentally related illnesses like black lung, thyroid cancer, and emphysema. Poverty, insufficient health care, and poor education are also a part of the tragic mix. Yet despite these problems, many in this region still hold on to a very healthy optimism that rests on the importance of loyalty to God, family, and community. One can still find men and women here who to a considerable extent live off the land, whether through their meticulously tended gardens, their reliance on hunting to supplement the family larder, or their intimate knowledge of the medicinal properties of various indigenous plants. The church is also of vital importance, providing the kind of intimate community support so often lacking in the double-wide sanctuaries of the American suburbs.

It was in Appalachia that I began to read the Hebrew and Christian scriptures anew, seeking always, in the manner of Gutiérrez and others, to temper my theological reflections with my primary vocation of addressing in my praxis the injustices that have been endured in these mountains. This involved not only hearing the stories of people whose families have lived here for generations but also listening to the language of the fields, gardening in a clay soil from which the blood of Abel seemed perpetually to cry out. Reading the scriptures with this Appalachian dirt on my hands, I inevitably arrived at the observations that have already been elaborated in chapter 4 about Adam and his progeny, his original vocation as a tiller and keeper, and Cain's dwelling in the land of Nod.

More importantly, it was impossible for me to conceive of any satisfactory answer to the lawyer's question as long as I continued to see the world through anthropocentric lenses. Here my neighbors were as varied as the Indigo Bunting who sang from the top of the same white pine every morning, the ginseng whose leaves were the first to turn a golden yellow in the fall, and my friend Mary Lou, who would offer her herbal remedies whenever someone in the community was ill. Each of these experiences, and so many more, helped me to arrive at the most fundamental principle of any theology of place: I am who I am by virtue of where I am. My life-place must therefore be included in my reflections on the extent of my moral community, the place where I am called to do my tilling and keeping. To a certain extent, then, ecology determines ontology. Thus, thinking locally is as important to radical (literally "rooted") theology as it is to radical economics.

Addressing the task of expanding liberation theology to include much more than simply one's social context, I propose

three basic theses. My assumptions, however, are not too far removed from those that lie at the center of any theology of liberation, namely, that God has a preferential option for the poor,
that theological reflection must occur "only at sundown," and
that any theology abstracted from a particular context runs the
risk of becoming not only irrelevant but a potential tool of oppression. At the same time, I am not willing to renounce entirely
the Western theological tradition that has for decades informed
my thinking about God, creation, and humanity. My theses, arrived at through a relatively novel form of liberating engagement
with a particular life-place, reflect my understanding of a God
who is at once a personal, redemptive, and sustaining presence
who can become uniquely manifest in a local biotic community. Thus, the theology of place elaborated here is Trinitarian
in its structure and corresponds to our discussion in chapter 1
of three terms I have alluded to throughout this book: spirituality, community, and sustainability.

God as Personal Presence

It will be important at the outset to affirm explicitly what I have
been implying all along: the orthodox conception of God's transcendence will have to be critically revised if it is to be relevant
to the experience of encountering the Divine uniquely in one's
place. Again, an overemphasis on the Priestly account of creation is partially to blame for our understanding of God as distant from the earth, as one who speaks a world into existence
and observes it from afar. God's essence has been similarly conceived as aloof, to such an extent that even the very nature of
God—love (1 John 4:8)—has often been qualified on the basis
of its perfection. In contrast to the apparently imperfect, self-
interested human emotion, God's love—*agape*—is uninterested,
or so the philosophically derived reasoning of the past would
have us believe.

An omnipotent, omniscient, immutable, impassive Creator, the
traditional theologians tell us, cannot be moved or compelled to
love (despite the wealth of evidence to the contrary in both the

Hebrew and Christian scriptures). This doctrinal truth only creates more problems when women and men, the *imago dei*, make this the ultimate model for their own compassion toward others. As history demonstrates, they have been more prone to arrive at and justify their concern for their neighbor based not on an appeal to empathy or fellow feeling but rather on principles rationally—objectively—derived. As God observes disinterestedly the *object* of God's love from afar, so must humans created in this image do the same. This love cannot help but remain on its own front porch.

Our theological reflections, then, must bracket the received notion of a theistic God and turn to a tradition that has always lingered just below the conscious surface of orthodox Christianity. In contrast to theism, we need to rely on a panentheistic understanding of God, where all things live and move and have their being *in* the divine. This is not to say, however, that all things are God, for no one entity or collection thereof is capable of fully encompassing or revealing the divine mystery. In panentheism, God can more justifiably be referred to as at one and the same time immanent (for all things are in the divine) and transcendent (God is inevitably greater than any one entity or the sum of all entities). This perspective is especially preferable to traditional theism with respect to its implications for ethics. As we have seen with Native American cultures, concern for the other is much more earnest when an appeal can be made to a reality that both parties hold in common, whether this be the Great Spirit, or its Christian variants, the Ground of Being or the Eternal You. Even the act of seeing is affected: "distance as space between is collapsed. Communication [becomes] direct and immediate."[11] With such a paradigm, concern for the other must necessarily include a concern for the self; though the two are distinct, they share a common essential source. Thus, my face—who I am as an individual—is inevitably connected to, and to some extent created by, my place, my community.

Though panentheistic theology has been expounded by a number of philosophers and theologians throughout the centuries—most notably Plotinus, John Scotus Eriugena, and Nicholas of

Cusa—I have been most inspired by one of its more erudite modern proponents, Martin Buber (1878–1965). In 1923, Buber offered to the world what many believe to be the essence of his thought: a little book titled *Ich und Du* (translated into English in 1937 as *I and Thou*). Central to this work is the notion that there are basically two ways that we as self-conscious beings relate to our world. The first, for Buber, is the way of freedom and relationship; the second, which is characteristic of our age, is ultimately the way of loneliness.

> The attitude of man is twofold in accordance with two basic words he can speak.
> The basic words are not single words but word pairs.
> One basic word is the word pair I-You.
> The other basic word is the word pair I-It; but the basic word is not changed when He or She takes the place of It. . . .
> Basic words are spoken with one's being [*Wesen*].
> When one says You, the I of the word pair I-You is said, too.
> When one says It, the I of the word pair I-It is said, too.
> The basic word I-You can only be spoken with one's whole being.
> The basic word I-It can never be spoken with one's whole being.[12]

Thus may the entirety of Buber's short treatise—indeed, the whole of his theological anthropology—be summarized, however cryptically.

It is significant that Buber introduces his work by suggesting that essential human existence is best represented by word pairs, for the foundation of his philosophy is the notion that "in the beginning is the relation."[13] For Buber, having been influenced by the witness of the Jewish prophets, a person is defined by the various encounters that he or she has perpetually with the world and with God. Along with Barth, Buber could affirm that

I *am* by virtue of my relationships. An individual cannot be abstracted from his or her context; there are no genuine subjects who stand alone. All are participants in the reality of God, who is the source of all being. Thus, there can be no true "I" objectified and removed from the rest of the world, only an "I" in relationship with another.

Buber's cosmos is thus characterized first and foremost by dialogue; it is a universe that is comprehensible and meaningful only through encounter. He is able to conceive such a world because he is, on the one hand, deeply influenced by his Jewish understanding of God as personal and, on the other hand, closely allied with the Platonic mystical tradition that enamored him in his early years. In contrast to the ego related to things—that is, the modern conception of the individual existing in the world—Buber offers the idea of the *person* who is only such when he or she enters into meaningful relationships with other subjects in his or her midst. This is the foundation of an authentic existence: I am only genuinely human through encounter, as I-You.

It is important to recognize that Buber's unique terminology—I and You—should not be construed to imply that relationships occur only on the human plane. This is where his theological emphasis is preferable to that of Barth, and even most liberationists. Yes, says Buber, the human realm is where the basic word becomes manifest in language, but there are in fact two additional spheres in which the Eternal You can become present, each lying just beyond the two horizons of human consciousness. The first potential encounter is with spiritual beings. "Here the relation is wrapped in a cloud but reveals itself, it lacks but creates language. We hear no You and yet feel addressed; we answer—creating, thinking, acting: with our being we speak the basic word, unable to say You with our mouth."[14] By contrast, lying just beyond the opposite pole of human consciousness is life with nature, where relation remains *below* language but is nevertheless intimated in the darkness. And it is here, I think, that Martin Buber has the most to offer as we seek to rediscover our moral sense of place.

Buber recognizes in a very practical way that our experience of nature is often unexceptional and routine. How quickly we take for granted the enchanting beauty of the mountains or the rolling streams we see everyday. How easily they become objects in our world. But there are moments, Buber suggests, when a person can hear in crisp tones the enigmatic language of the fields, can for a brief time—often just an instant—delve beneath the It-world and come face to face with the Eternal You. This can happen in any number of ways: an encounter with a house cat, for example, or with a dappled mare, even with a piece of mica. The Eternal You lies at the heart of all.

I contemplate a tree.

I can accept it as a picture: a rigid pillar in a flood of light, or splashes of green traversed by the gentleness of the blue silver ground.

I can feel it as movement. . . .

I can dissolve it into a number, into a pure relation between numbers and eternalize it.

Throughout all of this the tree remains my object and has its place and its time span, its kind and condition.

But it can also happen if will and grace are joined, that as I contemplate the tree I am drawn into relation, and the tree ceases to be an It. The power of exclusiveness has seized me.[15]

It is the sublime melancholy of our lot, however, that such experiences in human life are more often the exception than the rule, that even when we are fortunate enough to have them, these genuine encounters do not last long. Relationships quickly run their course, and the You becomes an It once again, becomes yet another object in the world. In other words, what is present to me now will inevitably lose its actuality and enter into thinghood again and again. Even love, says Buber, cannot exist in direct relation but must undergo this alternation between actuality and latency. Yet with this awareness we are able to recognize most keenly that we are living in a cosmos rife with possibility, replete with mystery, filled with objects that at any moment may, "if will and grace are joined," be addressed as You. And the source of this is a profound and abiding reality.

> In every sphere, in every relational act, through everything that becomes present to us, we gaze toward the train of the eternal You; in each we perceive a breath of it; in every You we address the eternal You, in every sphere, according to its manner. All spheres are included in it, while it is included in none.
>
> Through all of them shines the one presence.[16]

Personality may therefore be encountered in nature, for all creatures—from minerals to mammals—are grounded in the personal presence that is God.

Buber is especially helpful with respect to two aspects of our discussion so far. In the first place, he is able to elucidate what we all experience so acutely in the depth of our being in those moments when the Eternal You is hidden from us, as we, Adam's wayward children, live so disconsolately in the It-world. As the *imago mundi et dei*, our very essence requires that we be in relationship with the Eternal You and seek out encounters with this personal presence in every aspect of the world around us. We are, in other words, called to be our brother's keeper, our sister's seeker. Our being is dialogical at its core and best summarized by the word pair I-You. However, like Cain, we often seek our own autonomy, forsaking our essential nature and turning our backs on the possibility of encountering personalities in the world around us. We prefer, rather, to remain secure in the land of Nod, that is, to see these subjects perpetually as It or as objects with which we have only a causal relationship. There is little use, we tell ourselves, in even attempting to perceive things differently.

This is particularly true of the modern scientific approach to the world, in which persons, both human and nonhuman, are readily reduced to their constituent parts for the purpose of observation. In such a state, one must inevitably see oneself as yet another It, one more faceless object in a world devoid of meaning. Thus results the "sickness of our age," as Buber referred to it: held aloft by the rational abstractions of our scientific method, we now inhabit a cosmos where the possibility of encounter is all but eliminated. So we vainly turn inward, where the only remnants of the Eternal You appear to dwell. We seek out spirituality to the exclusion of relation, and with an unhealthy suspicion of all things "religious."

Buber offers a way out of this predicament, however, and this is the second reason why he is so important for our discussion. Though it is not his primary concern in *I and Thou*, Buber nevertheless places great emphasis on the gift of language, one of the unique tools of human dialogue and a primary means by which encounters with the Eternal You can be made manifest for the benefit of others in the human community. As God reveals Godself in particular ways, and in a variety of contexts, such revelations can and should be made known not through scientific discourse but through poetic narrative—stories or liturgies that offer a faithful intimation of the myriad faces in our midst. This is vitally important for the benefit of those for whom the word pair I-It has become oppressively immediate. As *imago mundi et dei*, the call to *poiesis*, creation, is a fundamental aspect of our vocation, a means by which we image the Creator by seeking to bring the personalities in our midst to presence for the purpose of community. Through our stories of encounter we are able to offer compelling and insightful allusions to the sacred and thus provide guideposts for others languishing in the loneliness of the It-world. These stories then become the lenses through which we understand and recognize value and meaning in our world, while acknowledging ourselves as characters in an enacted narrative. Faithfully sought out and retold, our stories become the traditions within which our spirituality—our abiding sense of the Eternal You manifest uniquely in our place— is practiced.

Having said this, it now becomes possible for us to interpret in a new light one of Adam's fundamental tasks in the Garden, that of naming the animals. Critics in recent years have rejected the hierarchical and anthropocentric emphasis in traditional understandings of this myth, in which Adam seems simply to ascribe names to the various creatures in his midst, as if describing mere objects. But if we read the story in the light of Buber's theological anthropology, we are presented with a more intriguing possibility: Adam is instead called to give voice to his encounters with the Eternal You as he experiences the divine in and through the faces in his place. Each discloses God's presence in a unique manner, but in a way that is below language. Adam's task is to bring what is "intimated in the darkness" into the light of day by giving it poetic form and this as a preliminary and necessary foundation to his tilling and keeping. And so must the human vocation be similarly conceived, albeit in a postlapsarian world.

Our fleeting encounters with the Eternal You must be preserved and passed on for those in our community through our oral and written traditions, as well as through other nonverbal means of expression: music, dance, the visual arts. As imagers of God, our vocation includes faithfully naming—that is, giving voice to—our encounters with the Eternal You in our place. Through our *poiesis*, our creative action, we share our intimations of the divine as experienced uniquely in our biotic community.

For Buber, bringing the You to presence is a special activity for which the human subject is uniquely suited. As imagers of God, we are called to be creators, or, more specifically (because our vocation can never be entirely abstracted from the Eternal You), cocreators. But this endeavor is less a science than an art. It is a means by which an individual

confronts a form that wants to become a work through him. . . . What is required is a deed that a man does with his whole being: if he commits it and speaks with his being the basic word to the form that appears, then the creative power is released and the work comes into being. . . .

Such work is creation. . . . As I actualize, I uncover. I lead the form across—into the world of It. The created work is a thing among things and can be experienced and described as an aggregate of qualities. *But the receptive beholder may be bodily confronted now and again.*[17]

It is tempting to read Buber's reflections here as referring only to the work of individual artists bringing to presence their encounters with the sacred as if in a vacuum. But it is important to remember that Martin Buber was first and foremost a prophet of community. Indeed, he cherished the arts in all their various forms, but for him the ultimate art, the preeminent work, was the creation of community—a place where the Eternal You can be encountered most fully. Community, it might be said, is a certain refuge for those plodding alone through the meaningless sands of the It-world. For Buber, therefore, the care of souls is inextricably linked to the care of soils. One's awareness of the Eternal You needs to be nurtured and encouraged in the context not of a universe but of a particular place whose peculiar creations—narratives, liturgies, music, rituals, art—are faithfully passed on from one generation to the next. These creations, rather than being stultifying doctrines allowing for no novelty whatsoever, are dynamic traditions open to change within certain parameters. In community, one will be much more likely to encounter the eternal and to see the faces that rise up to meet her or him in that place. In community, we can develop spiritually by nurturing an awareness of the Eternal You as it becomes manifest uniquely in our place. We will return to this subject in the final chapter in our discussion of Spirit as the sustaining breath of a biotic community.

Though difficult to comprehend on a first or even second read, Buber's *I and Thou* helps to illuminate what we are hearing from so many today who believe that fulfillment can be found in spirituality apart from religion. In the first place, it affirms the foundational intuition that a "mysterious Other" lies at the most profound depths of the universe and in all things, an Eternal You who is accessible apart from the religious institutions that seem, in so many instances, only to prevent the seeker from knowing the source. Further, though Buber affirms the personal nature of God, he nevertheless does not try to limit our experience by attributing overly anthropomorphic qualities and characteristics to the divine. Like Tillich he prefers to think of God less as "a being" than as "being itself," a theological move that is highly attractive to many these days who have suffered one or more social injustices at the hands of an authoritarian Father-God. The divine personality for Buber lies more in what the Eternal You makes possible for all of us: encounter with the other, such that the word pair I-It is replaced, however fleetingly, with an intimation of our truest nature and vocation.

The Eternal You is thus the fundamental ground or condition for the possibility that we might become fully aware that, at our core, we are persons-in-dialogue able to utter the word pair I-You with the entirety of our being. In short, Buber's God helps us fully to recognize that the faces of our neighbors, human and nonhuman, are very much like our own. They call us to respond authentically, in reciprocity and love, from the ground of being shared by all. Thus, the first affirmation of our theology of place is that the Eternal You offers in every circumstance, every moment of our day, the invitation to realize our essential calling as *imago mundi et dei*.

We are left now to address perhaps the most pertinent question of all: How is it that these ideas can be conceived as peculiarly Christian? Thus far we have reflected on the writings of a Jewish philosopher and theologian and have not considered the one figure around whom all things must necessarily revolve if our theology is to be consistent with, or relevant to, the Christian tradition. What steps need to be taken before we can claim that what we are proposing here is more than just philosophical or theological in nature, but is in fact distinctively Christological? More specifically, what role do the life and teachings of Jesus of

Nazareth play in all of this? The answer lies in the very notion that Buber himself found so compelling: religious community.

Christ as Redemptive Community

As we begin this section, it will be important to remember that our ensuing discussion must not fall into the ever-present trap of assuming that our use of the term "community" refers only to an aggregate of human beings living and seeking out meaning on the plane of history, irrespective of place. We have seen how this has had detrimental effects not only on our understanding of ourselves as *imago dei* but also on the many landscapes that we and our theological forebears have inhabited.

As we saw in the previous chapter, Scripture attests to a much more holistic understanding of humans as bearers of God's image. This refers less to some essential nature that we share in common with the Creator—such as rationality—than to the task that we are commanded to perform in our place. We are to be imagers of God, tillers and keepers, an identity that is most perfectly attained when we freely encounter as You the faces—human and nonhuman—in our midst. This being the case, it is therefore impossible to think about human salvation apart from the redemption of the created world—and more specifically, our place—of which we are an integral part. This understanding of reconciliation with God is attested in both the Hebrew and the Christian scriptures.

In his Epistle to the Romans, the Apostle Paul makes a curious allusion. Throughout the first seven chapters of the letter he admonishes the faithful of Rome to attend to what appear to be rather individualistic concerns: do not fall victim, he exhorts, to the temptations of idolatry (Rom. 1:18-32); recognize that all persons are guilty before God and deserving of judgment (2:1—3:20); affirm that the sinner's justification, as the story of Abraham demonstrates, is not in works but through faith (3:21—5:11); believe in the efficacy of the atoning death of Christ (5:12); and be assured that no good resides in "the flesh" but only in "the Spirit of life in Christ Jesus" (7:1—8:17). It is easy to assume from all of this that Paul's primary focus is on personal piety pursued at the expense of the things of this world. But then we are introduced to an image that seems at first to be an anomaly. The concern turns quickly away from the wretched condition of women and men to the certain hope, not of the individual exclusively, but of creation as a whole:

> I consider that the sufferings of this present time are not worth comparing with the glory about to be revealed to us. For the creation waits with eager longing for the revealing of the children of God; . . . the creation itself will be set free from its bondage to decay and will obtain the freedom of the glory of the children of God. We know that the whole creation has been groaning in labor pains until now; and not only the creation, but we ourselves, who have the first fruits of the Spirit, groan inwardly while we wait for adoption, the redemption of our bodies. For in hope we were saved. (Rom. 8:18-19; 22-24)

What are we to make of this? Why this little excursus on creation in the context of a discourse about what it means to live faithfully in "the Spirit of life in Christ Jesus"?

In contrast to some scholars who have maintained that this passage refers to a dramatic, eager longing on the part of all the world for some future goal—that, as C. K. Barrett proposes, "[Paul] is not concerned with creation for its own sake"[18] but for the sake of the future redemption of Christians—I would suggest that this seemingly obscure reference cannot be fully understood apart from the paradigm that we have been considering above. Indeed, it is entirely consistent with our ecostential (as opposed to existential) exposition of the Fall: as all of creation suffers the consequences of Adam's sin, and of Cain's alienation, so should all of creation be redeemed when humans as *imago mundi et dei* reclaim their place in the cosmos as children of God, and profess once again their calling as imagers of the Creator. Only then may creation give birth to authentic being, for humans will have turned their faces away from their tendency to make Cain's story their own and toward a fulfillment of their true vocation as tillers and keepers, cocreators bringing to presence the Eternal You in their place.

This is redemption, not merely for the dispossessed individual, but also for the *place* where that person lives. This, I would suggest, is how we must think about living "in the Spirit of life in Christ Jesus." In light of our current ecological embarrassments, we must begin to consider Christian redemption less in terms of the individual's reconciliation with God and more in terms of an experience of *reconciliatory emancipation* in one's place. Redemption, then, becomes the freedom experienced when the I turns his or her face away from an obsession with the It-world and toward the You abiding in his or her midst, eliminating as much as possible the distance between and among all members of the community. With this conception of redemption in mind, we will need also to reconsider our traditional emphasis on salvation history—the story of God's salvific acts on the plane of time. We now need a much more inclusive alternative, one that has always lingered just below the theological surface in the West: *salvation ecology*—that is, the experience and proclamation of redemption in place, where one lives and breathes and has his or her being.

But does this mean that we will have to set aside the customary focus on the life and teachings of the person Jesus of Nazareth and reflect rather on his existence as "the Cosmic Christ," as some have recently suggested?[19] There are certain advantages to this approach, not least of which is an implicit sacramentalism that in the last four centuries has been too little emphasized apart from the Anglican, Roman Catholic, and Greek Orthodox traditions. When we affirm along with Paul that "all things have been created through [Christ] and for [Christ] . . . and in him all things hold together" (Col. 1:16-17), we can no doubt come to appreciate a sacred presence in the cosmos that establishes the created order as an outward sign of God's grace. The world thus becomes worthy of our moral consideration.

But unfortunately this perspective suffers from the same weaknesses found in Teilhard's cosmology: the personality of Christ becomes lost in the vastness of the universe, and his proximity there becomes yet another abstraction. Thus, the particularity of our individual lives, and that of the unique communities in which we live, pales in comparison to the grand, Christological scheme of things. We cannot fully reconcile this approach with what we know and affirm about the compassionate man Jesus of Nazareth, whose concern for the intrinsic value of even the lowliest members of Galilean and Judean society is a central theme throughout the Gospels. Intuitively we feel a much stronger sense of commitment to the person who with his finger drew pictures in the dust than to "the image of the invisible God, the firstborn of all creation" (Col. 1:15). We feel a much stronger sense of commitment to a Christ with a face.

On the other hand, we certainly do not want to err on the side of the particularity of Christ, as do many these days who feel compelled always to refer to Jesus as their "*personal* Lord and Savior," a man whose death and resurrection have saved *me* from *my* sin. This hyper-individualism only obscures the fact that, as both the Hebrew and the Christian scriptures make quite evident, God loves *the world*, not merely God's image on earth (John 3:16). The "monogrammed Jesus" approach to interpreting the Gospels and the Epistles of Paul commits the very sin of anthropocentrism that has landed us in our present predicament, focusing on individual human redemption to the exclusion of all other creatures, often suggesting that this world itself is that from which we need most urgently to be saved.

Furthermore, as Elisabeth Schüssler Fiorenza and others have noted, the androcentric (male-centered) bias of the Bible, which has served throughout the history of the church to uphold patterns of male supremacy and misogyny, is only reinforced by an undue emphasis on the gender of the Son of God.[20] Even if Jesus is portrayed as a vocal opponent of all forms of hierarchy and patriarchy, as he well should be, he is nevertheless male, and when the central figure of the Christian religion is conceived as such, women are forced necessarily, by virtue of their gender, to identify themselves as "other." A male-dominated God language and the incarnation of the Divine in the man Jesus, many feminists argue, only serve symbolically and actually to disempower women. Therefore, an overemphasis on the particularity of Jesus may in practice be counterproductive to the Christian ideals of human liberation and reconciliation, not to mention its antipathy to a concern for the redemption of our biotic communities. We need, therefore, a middle way.

In his book *Remembering Esperanza* Mark C. Taylor offers a helpful alternative to focusing on either the particularity or the universality of Christ and provides direction for our elaboration of what it means to live "in the Spirit and life of Christ Jesus." Taylor argues that what is most needed in the Christian community today is an empowering mythos that will serve to deliver us from the oppressive circumstances assailing us on all sides: sexism, ethnocentrism, classism, racism, heterosexism. Though he admits that at times he feels the urge to be done with Christianity entirely, he nevertheless holds fast to the germ of hope that lies dormant in the narratives of the tradition, however small this germ may be. Taylor has resolved to work within the religious structures that have informed his worldview and ethics from early childhood. But the narratives of the tradition, he argues, need now to turn away from their customary emphasis on the person, Jesus of Nazareth, and focus rather on the example of Jesus' lifework, what we might call his "imaging of God."

In other words, we need now to affirm that the power of the Christian mythos resides not so much in who Jesus was—the incarnation of God—but in the recognition that Jesus' individuality and commitments were in fact part of a larger community whose creative activity was greater than any set or sum of actions on the part of its members. Jesus was a participant, though a vitally important one, in a *sociohistorical dynamic*, the distinctiveness of which was its focus on a singular objective: reconciliatory emancipation among all members of the group—insiders and outsiders.

Having said this, the importance of a new narrative becomes clear. "The empowering mythos we need," Taylor suggests, "is not only a mythos displaying, telling, and retelling the story of an individual hero, Jesus. It needs to become, more than the tradition has allowed it to become, a mythos of Jesus *and* other lives touching and contributing to his as he touches and contributes to theirs."[21] In this new story Jesus the man should be recognized as the necessary fermenting ingredient—the leaven—in the sociohistorical gestalt of which he was a part, a presence permeating and enlivening the whole through his interaction with other personal agents: "other men and women, other social, cultural, and political forces."[22] Certainly without his commitments to the ideals of inclusion, his table fellowship with sinners, his teaching, his death, and every other facet of his remarkable life, there would have been no movement to speak of in first-century Palestine. But Jesus did not work in a vacuum, and this is the point that we need most to emphasize. As the preeminent example of the *imago mundi et dei*, he was who he was by virtue of where he was.

Rita Nakashima Brock suggests another elemental image to describe the relationship between Jesus and his social context. In *Journeys by Heart: A Christology of Erotic Power*, Brock argues along similar lines that the life-giving power, the lifework, of Jesus' sociohistorical community should be emphasized over the particularity of the man:

> Jesus is like a whitecap on a wave. The whitecap is momentarily set off from the swell that is pushing it up, making us notice it. But the visibility of the whitecap, which draws our attention, rests on the enormous pushing power of the sea—of its power to push with life-giving labor, to buoy up all lives, and to unite diverse shores with its restless energy. . . . Jesus' power lies with the great swells of the ocean without which the white foam is not brought to visibility.[23]

In other words, Jesus the man becomes the representative focal point of a liberative venture that is taking place between God and a particular community in the world, as well as among all members of this community.

Brock's metaphor is able to lend depth and meaning to our theology of place in a way that Taylor's "leaven" does not. Despite his very authentic concern for reconciliatory emancipation, Taylor, like so many of the liberationists who have influenced him, remains far too anthropocentric in his Christological reflections. He suggests that the gestalt of which Jesus the man was an integral part was merely a "sociohistorical dynamic" consisting of "other men and women, other social, cultural, and political forces." In other words, "the Spirit of life in Christ Jesus" occurs, in his estimation, on the plane of history, in the interaction of *human* personal agents sharing a common goal; their *place* seems to be of little or no concern. His ecological sensibility, therefore, is a kind of "half-way covenant," focusing simply on the interdependence of humans.

Brock, on the other hand, provides an image that is much more consistent with our understanding of the face of God arising from the depths of Being, cresting in a particular figure whose identity is dependent not simply on a sociohistorical dynamic, but on the *ecological* community of which he is a part. Jesus did not interact exclusively with men and women and other social forces; he was also a product of the very soil of Galilee itself. He spoke in parables employing images from his natural surroundings. He kept an ear open to the language of the fields, the birds of the air, the sheep and goats of the Galilean countryside, the seed sown in various types of soil. He was nourished both physically and spiritually by the land around him; the story of his place was to a certain extent *his* story.

What made Jesus unique was his acute awareness of the myriad faces that rose up to meet him in his place and his desire to be their keeper, as it were, by offering each of them the hope of reconciliation and the freedom of authentic existence. Aware of his original calling as an imager of God, he sought always to bring their distinctive reality to presence through the words of his parables and through his acts of kindness and healing. We might say, in the manner of Buber, that he perpetually revealed the Eternal You to those in his midst who languished in the dull loneliness of the It-world. Like the prophet Micah, he raised the hope that a messianic community, the Kingdom of God, was being established in their very midst, a place where men and women would beat swords into plowshares and where none would make them afraid. In Jesus, the peaceable kingdom was at hand, for he was the superlative example of the *imago mundi et dei.*

Far from thinking of him as merely a sociohistorical dynamic, then, we should begin now to think of Christ not only as the anointed *one* on whom the spirit of God rested, with whom God was well pleased, but also, and perhaps primarily, as a *natural-historical dynamic* whose fundamental objective is reconciliatory emancipation among *all* members of a place, human and non-human. This, then, is the body of Christ: any ecological community whose lifework is reflective of the very tilling and keeping that lie at the center of salvation ecology. Wherever we find a group of people living according to the expectations of the land, listening to the language of their fields, regarding themselves merely as plain members, experiencing consciously (though not necessarily cognitively) both the actual unity (reconciliation) and the actual diversity (emancipation) present among all creatures in their place, and facilitating the perfect, unobstructed effusion of love between I and You, there we find the Divine become manifest. Christ, therefore, is neither cosmic nor particular but a mediation of the two: Christ is a *biotic community* in which meaningful being becomes incarnate as "being-with," that is, as the experience of having entered into mutually affirming relationships with the others who share my life-place.

It should not go without saying that this conception of Christ as an ecological community of reconciliatory emancipation has the added advantage of drawing our attention away from the particularity of the man, Jesus, and thus away from one of the more evident aspects of his identity: his maleness. As mentioned earlier, many women have found the image of a salvific God who becomes incarnate in an individual man a very difficult concept to adopt as their own. The hierarchical understanding of the God-human relationship promoted by the exclusivity of the male God and male savior has served in the past to exclude women from full participation in both communion and leadership of the body of Christ. Thus a certain cognitive dissonance has to be endured by more than half the members of any church congregation: the "good news" of liberation and salvation in the male Christ is not made manifest in the very practical experiences of women who help to make up the body of Christ.

If Christ is recognized less in terms of the man Jesus of Nazareth, the incarnation of God, and more along the lines of the lifework exemplified in this particular person-in-community—a manner of being and doing that was marked by inclusiveness, as evidenced in his table fellowship—then we can begin to breathe a little easier, for it is conceivable that this salvific gestalt could be made known just as easily through a female as through a male metaphor. Reconciliation and emancipation are not gender-specific. With this new paradigm all persons—all genders—are capable of pursuing their true vocations as imagers of God, bringing into being the compassionate and liberating presence of the Eternal You in their place.

In contrast to the received dogma of the church, we must now profess that the incarnation of Christ is in no way a once for all, static reality, nor will it ever be the same in all places and at all times. Just as in recent years scientists and environmentalists alike have come to recognize the importance of bioregionalism—defining a particular area of the world not according to its historical and sociopolitical features but according to its distinctive ecology—so must theologians now be open to and conversant with the idea of "Christo-regionalism." Christ, no longer either particular or cosmic, is nevertheless both universal and unique in that Christ becomes that place where, in the words of Gerard Manley Hopkins, "the just [one] justices" in the midst of a biotic community anointed in the oil of righteousness and liberation. This being the case, we can also say, along with Hopkins, that "Christ plays out in ten thousand places."[24] The universality of Christ lies in the reconciliatory and emancipatory nature of the gestalt that can occur *in any place*, for the Eternal You is present, according to Buber, "in every sphere." The uniqueness is in the peculiar lifework or discipline necessary to make these ideals manifest in each biotic community. The lifework that reveals Christ will be quite different in the hills of Appalachia, for instance, than in the desert habitat of New Mexico. This playing out occurs in innumerable bioregions across the United States, and across the globe, whenever humans in their particular places recognize and affirm the profound relationship between what makes them distinct and valuable persons—that is, their free responses to the call of God, their faces—and the "ecological wave" upon which each of them crests creatively— their place. The two are not autonomous but mysteriously, sacramentally one. Faces arise out of places.

In all times and in all bioregions there have been those whose perception of the reconciling and liberating character of their natural-historical gestalt has been particularly keen, individuals who, like whitecaps on the ocean, are momentarily set off from the swell that pushes them up and whose words and actions become paradigmatic for the larger community. Jesus of Nazareth was such a figure (indeed, he is *the* paradigmatic person-in-community), a man whose God-consciousness was so acute that both his teachings and the example of his lifework inspire and direct the lives of millions of Christians today. But others could be mentioned here. In our own American experience we might refer to those peculiar prophets of the land who have been featured throughout this study: Aldo Leopold, living and working as a plain member of the sand counties of northern Wisconsin; Wendell Berry, farming and writing in his native central Kentucky; Wes Jackson, working in the tall-grass prairie ecosystem of southeastern Kansas. The future of the church, I believe, requires that we now begin to recognize not only the centrality of the life and teachings of the man Jesus of Nazareth but also the similarly inspired efforts of these people in place.

Their work has not been merely scientific, political, or aesthetic in nature; it has been Christological in scope.

This brings us once again to Paul's rather cryptic reference to the revealing of the children of God for which the creation waits with eager longing. Indeed, the image is much more explicit than this: creation is compared to a woman laboring through the pangs of childbirth, "groaning in travail," as if the infamous curse of Eve were felt in the very womb of the earth itself. By what midwifery will this new creation be brought into the world? According to the paradigm proposed above, by nothing less than a sincere affirmation that we are indeed the *imago mundi et dei* whose fundamental vocation, the faithful tilling and keeping of our place, might one day—if will and grace be joined—reestablish "the former dominion" (Mic. 4:8). Reconciliation among all members of the body of Christ—human and nonhuman—will be the beginning of what Paul alludes to as "the glorious liberty of the children of God." Separation as space between, a fundamental staple of the It-world, will be seen for the illusion that it is, and "nation shall not lift up sword against nation, neither shall they learn war any more" (Isa. 2:4; Mic. 4:3). But this will not be a once-for-all activity. Like tilling and keeping itself, as well as the locally defined practice of the liberationists, reconciliation is a perpetual process.

With this understanding of the messianic community, we could not be any further removed from the apocalyptic hopes of many premillennial Christians who await the return of Christ through so many cataclysmic events. The coming of Christ is not here accompanied by trumpet blasts and the rattling of swords, but rather by the still small voice that consoled the prophet Elijah during his desert retreat (1 Kings 18). It comes not so much as a thief in the night but as the unfolding of a tiny mustard seed: slowly, imperceptibly, yet with extraordinary results. And in this growth we as tillers and keepers cannot sit idly by and hope that God will one day bring creation to its final catastrophic end. On the contrary, we must act in our place, informed by our unique sense of who we are and by the example of the lifework of Jesus. We are cocreators, assured that in our tilling and keeping both divine grace and human will are mysteriously joined and that through this union the spirit of our place (what Leopold called its "integrity") can and will be creatively sustained.

We are left now to consider the third aspect of our proposed theology of place: the sustaining role of the Holy Spirit. In this chapter we have been moving from a consideration of God to the community of Christ, and in so doing we have narrowed our focus as we have proceeded. The Eternal You, it was suggested, makes possible the intimation of the sacred on the part of an individual, regardless of his or her community involvement or setting. For this reason this conception of the divine is highly attractive to those who prefer "spirituality" to "religion," the latter usually being associated with some institutional structure. In our consideration of Christ as a biotic community of liberation, however, our focus narrows, and the form of what some might call "religion" comes into view. We are no longer dealing only with an intimation of the divine in the universe but with the unfolding presence of God in a particular biotic community, and this for an expressed purpose: reconciliation and liberation among all members of the community.

These principles, in other words, "tie back" one's experience of the Eternal You, directing it to a stated end. The next chapter's discussion of the Holy Spirit as God's sustaining breath experienced uniquely in a place will serve further to refine this "religious" move of adding structure to one's spiritual encounter with the divine. It will also provide the starting point from which members of the body of Christ can develop a discipline for knowing and communicating God's presence in a particular biotic community.

6

Learning the Language of the Fields

Telling Stories

Throughout the preceding chapters we have considered the role that stories play in shaping the way cultures create value and meaning in the world. Among the indigenous peoples of North America, myths about emergence from the womb of the earth helped those who recounted these narratives to establish a sense of kinship with the nonhuman inhabitants of their life-world. But myths can also be destructive in their effect, as we saw with the stories told among Euro-American immigrants to the New World. The assurance that humans alone were created in the image of God and thus could exercise dominion over creation set the stage for the abuse of the land on which the newcomers settled, not to mention the exploitation of its human and non-human inhabitants.

In light of this dual role, it is important always to keep the power of myth under a watchful eye and to offer narratives that challenge and critique the dominant worldview created by our stories. Among Native Americans, trickster tales serve this purpose, reminding those who hear them that the reality they perceive through their myths is nonetheless vulnerable to disruption, that disorder is as much a part of their waking day as the order they have come to know and expect. In the Judeo-Christian tradition the role of "trickster," if we may use this term, is equally important, as seen in the words and deeds of the Hebrew prophets and most clearly in the life and teaching of the paradigmatic person-in-community, Jesus of Nazareth. Jesus was profoundly aware of the mythology of his day that featured the coming of a messiah who would set the affairs of the world aright for the Jewish nation. But Jesus also perceived how this perennial hope had become a kind of stumbling block to the true calling of God's people, encouraging them to look for a worldly kingdom that featured all the trappings and excesses of their Roman oppressors. So he told his own stories and even acted them out in his life and death. This should not be overlooked as Christians today seek out ways to live as alternative communities of hope and liberation in the midst of a world dominated by a prevailing global mythology.

Jesus knew how to capture imaginations with his words and illustrations. This feature of his ministry accounts for his overwhelming popularity among the *'am ha-aretz*, the people of the land, and it certainly sheds light on the disdain he evoked among those in positions of authority. His disputations with the scribes and the Pharisees were less forays into the esoteric nuances of scripture interpretation than opportunities to speak prophetically in parables and thereby challenge the status quo of Galilean and Judean society. John Dominic Crossan, in his now-classic text *The Dark Interval*, offers important insights into the radical nature of Jesus' storytelling and explains how narratives told in communal settings serve both a constructive and a deconstructive function.[1] Crossan suggests that all stories can be conceived as falling somewhere along a continuum extending between two complementary poles. On the one end are myths, whose primary purpose is to offer mediation between what appear to be irreconcilable opposites encountered regularly in one's life-world. As we have seen, myths provide the deep structure that enables humans to attribute meaning to their experience, but they also engender hope and optimism, the assurance that "all things work together for good." Religious traditions across the world could not flourish without some form of mediating narrative to assuage the fears and doubts of the faithful. Yet myths also bring with them a danger that must be exposed: they can serve as blinders that prevent us from acknowledging so many tragic aspects of human existence. They too often provide the occasion for us to ignore lived reality in favor of a comforting fantasy.

This point can perhaps best be illustrated by a brief reference to the work of René Girard, whose extensive social scientific research over the last several decades has focused on the "myth of redemptive violence."[2] We are all familiar with the outlines of this story: A community experiences a threatening disruption in its social fabric and interprets this as a sign of divine displeasure. The situation can only be remedied—or so say the cultic powers that be—by the sacrifice of one identified as the source of the problem. Through the violent death of the scapegoat, the gods are appeased, and the world of chaos becomes ordered once again. Reconciliation takes place through the public ritualization of the myth, and more specifically through the brutal execution of the other. The people are mollified, the powers are preserved, and all for the relatively meager price of a single sacrifice. Girard maintains that variations on this theme can be found in cultures in every part of the world.

Mediating myths such as these, while attractive for their pacifying effects, nevertheless have the potential to become manipulative and oppressive in their telling. When this happens, those hearing the narrative are prevented from confronting the reality of their lived experience. The stories told among European settlers in the New World, featuring a God who was pleased with their subjugation of the chaotic wilderness, offer another case in point. The faithful were prevented from seeing the destruction they wrought, all the time believing their "improvements" to the land were the will of the Creator. And, to be fair, even the myth of a broken world restored to its original wholeness, where every person "reclines beneath the vine and the fig tree," runs a similar risk. So simply falling back on new and seemingly less exploitative narratives is not enough to answer the question of how a community can come to recognize and affirm the faces of so many others who also inhabit their place. It is therefore equally as important to speak as Jesus did, in parables.

According to Crossan, myths and parables are "binary opposites" that complement each other in their telling. While the former are concerned to create the belief in the permanent possibility of reconciliation, the latter are designed to challenge this mediation and in so doing alert the hearer to the fact that the world is never as intelligible as one's stories suggest. A parable reveals the seams and edges of an accepted myth; it is a "story grown self-conscious" of the limits of its possibility. Jesus' parable of the Good Samaritan, for example, effectively subverted the expectations of those who had grown complacent in their understanding of who was worthy to be affirmed as fully human and who was not. The two men in the tale who were seen as reconciled to God through their own merits—the priest and the Levite—were in fact the ones who were least worthy to be called "good." Indeed, it was the Samaritan, whom most hearers of this story would have regarded as exceedingly contemptible, who performed the fundamental task that God requires of all of us—caring for the neighbor.

Parables, then, reveal the chink in the armor of myth and hold open the possibility that God's ways might actually transcend what we can say about them through the stories we tell. Crossan quotes L. M. Vail to clarify this point: "In the openness of authentic disclosure we admit the possibility of something unknown, even contradictory, to our world; for we *put into question* our own faculties—for instance, reason, will, the sense—rather than blindly measuring and evaluating what is real on the basis of these."[3] What made the life of Jesus so significant, according to both Girard and Crossan, was his commitment to reveal in a prophetic way the underside of the myths that had debilitated the imaginations of so many in first-century Palestine. It is impossible for us to know fully the impact of Jesus' storytelling on those who heard him, but much of the radical nature of his parables continues to disturb us even today.

We still believe, for example, that laborers who give an honest day's work should be paid for their time and commitment; it is scandalous to suggest that men offering only a few hours in the fields should be awarded the same wage as those who have worked faithfully from dawn to dusk. And who among us does not identify with the loyal son seething as his father welcomes home his wayward brother? Jesus was the quintessential "parabler," to use Crossan's term; he told stories, but ultimately he became the story itself. His death on the cross at the hands of the Romans was, as Girard has indicated, the consummate act of subversion, enabling those who followed him, and those who would tell the tale ages hence, to experience for the first time in history the myth of redemptive violence *from the victim's perspective* and thus to expose it for the lie that it truly is. It is unfortunate that the early church lost sight of this powerful aspect of Jesus' death and substituted its own narrative of reconciliation, featuring a God whose justice could only be appeased by the blood of an innocent lamb. The fact that the Father, out of his divine mercy, offers his own Son as the perfect sacrifice does little to instill in the faithful the original insight of the Parabler's suffering on the cross—that, despite what the myth makers would have us believe, violence is never without its innocent victims, and it is rarely, if ever, redemptive.

Telling divine stories is important for shaping a sense of communal identity, but these must always move in dialectical fashion between the binary opposites of myth and parable, lest the former becomes reified and oppressive in its telling. Myths have too often been utilized as tools for maintaining the status quo; parables help us to see the mythic world from its underside, from the victim's perspective. As such, they need to be heard in every community whose focus is the emancipation and reconciliation of all persons in its midst. Our myths, in other words, need to be reminded from time to time to "make a place for Elijah," to leave our front doors slightly ajar in the hope that the prophetic other will reveal his or her face and join us at the table. We need perpetually to nurture the expectation that we can be surprised by new ways of seeing and thinking about our places.

Up to this point, we have focused primarily on the narratives that have been told about God and God's will for the world. But if we are honest with ourselves, we will admit that our concern for these too often pales in comparison to our preoccupation with a tale that lies much closer at hand: our own. Stories appeal to us on a very basic level because we cannot help conceiving our individual lives in narrative fashion. Our life stories are the means by which we reveal ourselves to others and create a personal sense of meaning and purpose. We arrive at an understanding of our own vocation less by philosophical speculation than by examining and appraising the narrative movement of our lives. But our stories also have the potential to conceal aspects of ourselves that we would rather not divulge, even to our closest friends. So, like myths, the personal tales we tell must include a sense of the parabolic, lest we become deluded into a misleading self-image. We also do a great disservice to both ourselves and our community if we fail to acknowledge that our individual narratives are in fact coauthored by so many others who share our life-world.

Given Charles Taylor's first malaise of contemporary culture—extreme individualism—it is easy to see how a hyper-personal story featuring "me and me alone" has come to occupy a dominant place in the minds of many, even to the exclusion of a divine narrative. But we are simply deceiving ourselves if the tales we tell of our journeys to this place do not include an elaborate cast of characters, both human and nonhuman, whose unique stories are also woven inextricably into the fabric of our own. For those of us who were raised in the church, this means acknowledging that the divine narrative has also played a significant role in our self-development and sense of identity.

In their book *Mighty Stories, Dangerous Rituals* Herbert Anderson and Edward Foley suggest that one of the great failures of the church in the twentieth century was its inability to connect the divine story with that of the individual, to help each person see himself or herself as an active part of a larger drama. While our worship has focused on introducing the faithful to God's creative and redemptive activity in the cosmos, pastoral care, by contrast, has tended to focus more on the individual's need to come to terms with his or her own story. In other words—if we can return here to Joseph Campbell's description of the four-fold structure of myth (see chapter 2)—the church has been adept at nurturing the mystical function of myth in its worship and the psychological function in its care of souls, but it has been unable effectively to incorporate the cosmological and sociological dimensions in the lives of the faithful. Consequently, the interdependent nature of the body of Christ has been so obscured that the divine narrative and the individual's life story are rarely able to be celebrated together in the life of the community.

Thus a despairingly wide gulf exists between the affirmation of God's mysterious presence in the cosmos and the recognition that this same spirit is at work in a meaningful way in *my* life. The priestly function of the community is therefore lost. If, as we suggested earlier, every human being as the image of God is Trinitarian by nature (that is, one's true sense of self can be found only in communion with God, self, and other), then it follows that spiritual wholeness can only be attained when all three stories— divine, individual, and that of my neighbor—can be heard and celebrated in unison. The three must not be understood as one, of course, lest the uniqueness of each be lost, but they can and should be acknowledged as "three hypostases," if you will, of the same essential myth of liberation and reconciliation.

Anderson and Foley believe that an effective means of bridging the gap between the divine and human narratives is through the celebration of new rituals. Building on the work of Ronald Grimes, they suggest that one place where the church has been particularly inattentive is in the provision of communally supported rites of passage for those suffering through life-changing events, like the miscarriage of a child or a debilitating illness.[4] Such transitions into new phases of a person's life are foundational to the stability and self-understanding of so-called primitive cultures, but the modern world seems to have little appreciation for rites of passage. Thus questions of identity and purpose abound in our society. This situation might change, however, with the introduction of new rituals, performed in the context of the community, that serve to integrate the divine story—celebrated in worship—and individual narratives—so often the focus of pastoral care. As Anderson and Foley indicate,

> the potential for a personally and communally transformative encounter is significantly magnified when the divine and human intersect in our storytelling and ritualizing. We are transformed in part because we begin to understand our particular story as part of a larger, transcendent narrative. God has chosen to coauthor a redemptive story for us and with us in human history, and in so doing has invited us to reshape radically the horizon of all other storytelling and ritual making.[5]

This new emphasis on ritual, it must be noted, makes a place for both the mythic and parabolic aspects of human and divine life, affirming these in the worship of the community. This is established primarily on the fundamental theological understanding of Jesus as one who achieves "mythic reconciliation in parabolic mode." It cannot be denied that the church has long affirmed the mediating character of the life, death, and resurrection of Jesus, such that peace with enemies and union with God are made possible. Thus the work of Jesus is ultimately mythic in its intent. But this can only be accomplished, Anderson and Foley point out, by first abandoning so many of the comfortable reconciliations that we have created for ourselves. Jesus must be understood as a "mythic parabler" and thus as a model for the stories we tell of our own lives in community. "While our preference might be the domestication of God, the embrace of the mythic, and the assertion of divine reconciliation at any cost, such an instinct must be challenged by the assertion of the parabolic in order to keep the paradox intact."[6] Narratives and rituals that do not maintain this precarious balance are apt to lose their prophetic power and become bland and routine.

Despite their keen insights into the narrative structure of human existence and the need for this to be affirmed in the communal life of the church, Anderson and Foley's perspective is not entirely adequate for helping us arrive at a more ecologically oriented understanding of what it means to live faithfully in our places. Though they have avoided falling victim to the global paradigm proffered by many theologians—indeed, they fully recognize, along with Robert Schreiter, that many congregations will inevitably construct "local theologies" as their stories are told—they are nevertheless short-sighted in their assessment of *whose* narratives can and need to be heard in the context of the community.[7] The quote above makes this evident: "God has chosen to coauthor a redemptive story with us and for us *in human history*" (emphasis added). While their perspective on the social location where our stories can be ritually affirmed is commendable, their assumption that only the divine and human narratives are relevant to their project belies a time-honored omission. The voices of the nonhuman others in our biotic communities need also to be heard.

Simply falling back on "local theology"—recognizing that the human story is coauthored by God and humans at a particular time in space—has the potential of perpetuating the traditional myth of salvation *history* in which creation is conceived as merely the stage upon which the human drama of redemption is played out. Ecological context is understood here as simply a prop for facilitating the confluence of the divine and human stories. If, however, we are going to affirm in a new way the Trinitarian nature of all humans as imagers of God living faithfully in place, then it will be necessary not only to celebrate the intersection of the divine and human stories in the life of the church, but also to affirm ritually the stories of the nonhuman others who similarly make up the body of Christ. These voices are not just embellishments on the more important drama that takes place between humans and God; they are valuable in their own right.

Thus the divine and human narratives, along with the long-ignored stories of our particular place, need to be heard together. In short, the "care of souls" in the life of the church must necessarily include the "care of soils," the tilling and keeping of the body of Christ. The narratives of God, humans, and *place* must all be heard from a new and liberating perspective: God has chosen to coauthor a redemptive story not only with us and for us in human history but also with the biotic community of which we are a part.

But herein lies the rub. If in the past the problem has been the attribution of value (determined by a prevailing, anthropocentric mythology) to the land of which Christians have been a part, then do we not here run a similarly destructive risk by suggesting that somehow we can connect our personal narratives with those of our place? Will we not inevitably fall back on our sinful tendency to ascribe to the nonhuman inhabitants of our community something that is not actually there, treating them as objects instead of subjects? How is it possible to hear their stories from a vantage point that is not inherently our own? How can we even begin to learn the enigmatic language of the fields? It is at this point in our discussion that we need to reconsider the way in which theologians have traditionally interpreted the person and work of the Holy Spirit.

Whereas in many traditions today the Spirit has been understood as the inspiration behind new ways of speaking, so as to spread the good news, in good global fashion, "to the ends of the earth," the opportunity now lies before us to emphasize the complementary aspect of this endeavor. The Holy Spirit, the breath of the Eternal You who vitalizes and sustains the body of Christ in its ecological particularity, is the one who helps us first to *listen*— to contemplate and perceive with a discerning ear the myriad voices speaking from the depths of our biotic communities. An integral aspect of our vocation as tillers and keepers is to bring these voices to presence, and this can be done by adopting a new variation on an old spiritual discipline.

Hearing the Language of the Spirit

Readers of the New Testament might be led to believe that any discussion of the Holy Spirit must begin with the promise that Jesus gave to his disciples at his ascension, a hope that came to fulfillment on the day of Pentecost. As Luke describes the event, the disciples were all gathered in Jerusalem, praying in one place, when

> And suddenly from heaven came the sound like the rush of a violent wind, and it filled the entire house where they were sitting. Divided tongues, as of fire, appeared among them, and a tongue rested on each of them. All of them were filled with the Holy Spirit and began to speak in other languages, as the Spirit gave them ability. (Acts 2:2-4)

Thus begins the story of "the dispensation of the Spirit," as it has been referred to in some circles. And there is a certain appeal to the narrative, filled as it is with supernatural occurrences and the implied promise that this same power of God can still work in similar ways among the faithful today. But what is often overlooked in many discussions of the Holy Spirit is the fact that this sometimes neglected person of the Trinity is by no means a latecomer on the scene of salvation ecology. On the contrary, the Spirit of God was present in the very beginning of time, hovering over the face of the waters, brooding, as it were, like a mother hen over her chicks.[8] It was this divine breath that formed the command "let there be . . . ," calling forth order and light out of the murky depths of chaos. The Nicene Creed is clear in its affirmation that the Holy Spirit proceeds equally from the Father and the Son, thus proclaiming that her role in the divine economy has both a creative and redemptive quality:

she is "creative redeemer," "redemptive creator," or, put more simply, "sustainer," one who enlivens and encourages the work of God even in the midst of a broken world.

Thus the advent of the Holy Spirit on the day of Pentecost is merely a continuation of her creative and sustaining work that is attested throughout the pages of the Hebrew scriptures. There the Spirit is seen as divine power and authority coming to rest on the anointed kings of Israel, a sign of God's good pleasure in God's chosen son. The prophets also describe occasions on which they are seized by this same spirit of the Lord and compelled to bring the Creator's will to presence through their poetic utterances and acts. "The Spirit of the Lord GOD is upon me," writes Third Isaiah, "because the Lord has anointed me; he has sent me to bring good news to the oppressed . . ." (Isa. 61:1). But God's immanence in the world is also affirmed in much less dramatic ways, particularly in those scriptural books and other writings that comprise the Wisdom Tradition. Here the creative and sustaining spirit of God is celebrated as working, even playing, in and through all things. The Psalmist makes it clear that there is indeed a *language* to be learned here, and words to be heard, as the spirit of the Holy One of Israel whispers, dances, and sings in every facet of the created world.

The heavens are telling the glory of God;
　　and the firmament proclaims his handiwork.
Day to day pours forth speech,
　　and night to night declares knowledge.
There is no speech, nor are there words;
　　their voice is not heard;
yet their voice goes out through all the earth,
　　and their words to the end of the world. (Ps. 19:1-4a)

Let those who have ears to hear, the Psalmist seems to say, acknowledge the presence of God's spirit in all things, whether human or nonhuman, animate or inanimate.

Having said this, it is important to recall Martin Buber's

assertion that the Eternal You can be encountered in every aspect of the natural world, but only in a way that is "beneath language." This does not mean, however, that what is being communicated by the nonhuman world—whether in the firmament or much closer to home in the eyes of a dappled mare—is altogether beyond the pale of our comprehension. On the contrary, it is indeed one of the fundamental responsibilities of each and every one of us to bring our admittedly rare encounters with the Eternal You to presence through our creative acts, and this for the good of the community yearning for a word of hope, for a sense of connectedness. We are called, in other words, to give voice to the unheard voices. Our creations toward this end—whether poetry, visual art, music, or even new and insightful rituals observed among the faithful—become the lenses through which our human community comes to recognize and understand value and meaning in their particular places, the means by which they acknowledge themselves as characters, or "plain members," in an ecologically enacted narrative.

What has been tragically forgotten over the millennia is that one of the most integral aspects of our human vocation is the careful listening required for perceiving these voices "going out through all the earth and to the end of the world." Simply put, the integrity of the body of Christ relies on the willingness and ability of its human members to affirm their most basic calling as tillers and keepers, imagers of God, by engaging in this new form of liberating "tongue speaking." We must endeavor to hear and proclaim faithfully the language of the fields coming to us from the depths of our place.

Though much has been made of the "pouring out" of God's Spirit on the day of Pentecost, it is instructive for us to consider a less conspicuous account of a similar event recorded in the Gospel of John. Here the Holy Spirit is bestowed on the followers of Jesus not from the heavens above with surging winds and descending tongues of fire but in a manner vaguely reminiscent of the Yahwist's creation narrative. Here the Spirit comes to the disciples intimately, from the very mouth of the risen Lord himself, who greets them face-to-face and offers a word of hope. As John relates the tradition,

> When it was evening on . . . the first day of the week, and the doors of the house where the disciples had met were locked . . . , Jesus came and stood among them and said, "Peace be with you." After he said this, he showed them his hands and his side. Then the disciples rejoiced when they saw the Lord. Jesus said to them again, "Peace be with you. As the Father has sent me, so I send you." When he had said this, he breathed on them and said to them, "Receive the Holy Spirit." (John 20:19-22)

If one reads this passage in the light of the Yahwist narrative in Genesis, one cannot help drawing parallels here between Adam and this "new creation," these believers, the body of Christ, whose vocation in the world is exactly that of their primal predecessor. The difference, however, is that here God's creative and redemptive presence—God's sustaining breath— awakens and inspires the disciples in a much more dynamic way. The same Spirit (Hebrew: *ruah*) who hovered over the face of the deep in the beginning, who invigorated the prophets of old and for millennia set creation to dance, now also quickens the body of the faithful, broken and inadequate though they are, and provides a renewed understanding of their most fundamental calling. The curse of the garden is reversed, and the connection with the earth is renewed. Indeed, this is the very event for which the creation had been waiting with eager longing, groaning in travail until the children of God would once again be revealed (Rom. 8:19). Before his ascension, Jesus, like God in the garden before him, creates the conditions for the possibility of a radically new kingdom on earth: he breathes the breath of life into the "new Adam," the church, and grants it peace—not so much as a parting blessing, but as a charge to the commencement of its liberating work in the world.

It is this same breath of God, rising from the depths of the

Eternal You through the body of Christ—that is, through our biotic community, wounded still in hands and side—who continues to energize and inspire us today. The Eternal You, who is "intimated in the darkness" of every aspect of our place, can be communicated to those who share our life-world, who can also encounter it directly through the creative movement of the Spirit herself. But the breath of God will not illuminate us in the same manner in every time and place, so our "tongue speaking," the creations of our hearts and minds that reveal the eternal, will also be as varied as the bioregions that make up our planet.

There is, then, no single language of the fields to be learned; to suggest as much is to fall victim to the very global thinking that is one of the sources of our ecological embarrassments. The spirit of the Eternal You, breathed through the body of Christ in its various ecological incarnations, creates a melody that can be heard in different tones and keys in each bioregion across the world. It is our calling as God's imagers first to hear the music and then to keep the song alive, to sustain the unique character— the integrity—of our biotic community, and thus to affirm the liberating movement of the Spirit there. And the voices of the nonhuman others *can be heard*, as Buber says, "if will and grace be joined." That is, their dulcet tones can present themselves to us if we are willing, as both individuals and as a community, to engage in the spiritual discipline of "careful listening," or what might best be described as a new *lectio divina*.

Those familiar with the ancient practice of *lectio* know that, despite its literal translation into English as "holy reading," the discipline is really more concerned with listening faithfully for the voice of God as it comes to us in sacred Scripture and in other religious texts. For those who commit to this daily exercise, *lectio* can provide an experiential encounter with God; in our reading, our own words and thoughts are willfully silenced so that the still small voice of the Creator can be discerned in the text before us. Of course, this practice is founded on certain very basic assumptions about who we are as human creatures and who God is as the One who addresses us through the

Word. As M. Basil Pennington has observed, *lectio* is an altogether meaningless endeavor for those who doubt that in reading Scripture we are immersing ourselves in the actual Word of God. Indeed, for this practice to be effective the Bible must be regarded in much the same way that an icon is understood in the Orthodox Church, as a sacred doorway offering us access to the Divine. Similarly, we must be willing to come to the text with a certain humility and an acknowledgment that an encounter with God is what we both want and need. Openness is also essential to the discipline; we should be receptive to the likelihood that what we experience in our holy reading may, like a parable, take us completely by surprise and upset the accepted contours of our safe and predictable life-world. Finally—and this is the point that so many of us in our busy lives are often unable to achieve—we must endeavor always to be faithful in our practice, to establish it as an authentic discipline, even though there will be times when our *lectio* will not appear to bear spiritual fruit.

All of this, Pennington notes, presumes an awareness and affirmation of who we are as unique individuals created in God's image. Our stories, our life narratives that have brought us to this place, play a significant role in how we perceive the voice of God coming to us through the text of Scripture.

> Each of us is a certain listening, a certain openness to being, to reality, to communication. Everything that has been a part of our lives since the moment of our creation has had its role in shaping the listening that we are. . . . It is as though my listening has a certain physical shape to it. As things come across my listening, I get only what falls within the parameters of the listening that I am.[9]

It is important to emphasize here that Pennington is not suggesting that our encounters with the Eternal You are sufficient in and of themselves to sustain us spiritually. He is not saying that we can be "spiritual but not religious." On the contrary, the act of careful listening must be carried out in the context of community so that others' experiences of God's voice, encountered in *lectio*, can also be heard. Sometimes these will affirm what we ourselves have discovered in our holy reading, in good mythic fashion; other times they will challenge it, in parabolic mode. But the important point is this: our listening should always be tempered by our humility. "In this humility, in this truth . . . I should want my own listening, the listening that I am, to be expanded. And I should want it to be complemented by the listening of others."[10]

According to the ancient tradition, *lectio divina* proceeds according to four interdependent steps: *lectio, meditatio, oratio,* and *contemplatio,* or, translated alliteratively and very loosely, "reading," "ruminating," "responding," and "resting." The first of these has been explained to some extent above: we come to the text of Scripture not so much for information or consolation but for insight into the mind of God, wanting to see the world as the Creator sees it. Pennington is even more explicit about what our intent should be: we approach the Word hoping to meet God as friend and intimate companion. In our careful listening to the lectionary passage for the day, in our slow and deliberate reading, we may encounter a word or phrase that strikes us as particularly apt or symbolic of our lives at this point in time. This is the place where our unique life experience meets the divine narrative in a poignant way. We read the word or phrase again, and then again, ruminating on its meaning, leaving the rest of the text for another day, another time. We allow our "word of life" to work as it will, undermining our customary assumptions about who God is and what God's will is for our community. God speaks to us as friend and provides insights into the divine life. When we have listened well, the time eventually comes for us to respond in gratitude: *oratio,* arising from the depths of our very being, is our thanksgiving for the gifts we have received. Buber might refer to this as a kind of speaking forth of the word-pair "I-Thou," bringing to presence in our own creative way the experience of our communion with the divine. Finally, we contemplate our relationship with God by simply "being with," by resting in God's holy presence. Like old friends or lovers grown accustomed to each other's silence, there is no longer a need for words. Pennington summarizes the process concisely: "As we listen to the Word (*lectio*), a word, a phrase, a sentence, may well strike us, and we let it reverberate within, opening and expanding, forming and shaping (*meditatio*), calling forth varied responses (*oratio*) until finally we simply rest in the Reality to which it all leads (*contemplatio*)."[11]

While *lectio divina* offers a time-honored means for encountering God in the texts of Scripture, it also provides a model for how we might better come to know the Eternal You in the myriad faces who rise up to meet us where we live. I have already suggested that organic gardening can be conceived as a kind of spiritual exercise, and thus as a practice on which we might reflect theologically. It can be, in effect, a kind of "holy reading." For the tiller and keeper who eschews all the ready-made horticultural shortcuts on the market today—the powerful fertilizers, the broadband herbicides, the hybridized seeds—the call to "listen carefully," to observe with a loving eye, is familiar indeed. So it takes little in the way of imagination to begin thinking about our gardening as a new kind of *lectio* practiced in the context of our place.

If we acknowledge that the spirit of God animates the body of Christ, the biotic community in which we strive in all things to engender emancipation and reconciliation, then we can also affirm that a certain reading, ruminating, responding, and resting in this place can and should reveal both the morally compelling faces of the others who inhabit our life-world and the face of the Eternal You who breathes on us, illumines us, from the depths of the body itself. Indeed, our work here is in many ways like the compulsion of the disciple Thomas upon meeting the resurrected Christ: we feel the need to place our hands into the wounds of the body before us—not in order to believe, but so that we might experience, and then begin to heal, the brokenness we find there. Soils destroyed by years of preventable erosion, biological diversity erased by centuries of domination and subjection, groundwaters contaminated by our continued insistence on chemical dependency: all of these cry out for restoration. There are indeed parables to be heard here, challenges to the easy reconciliations so often proffered by our technological mythology, but only for those who have ears to hear.

As above, our *lectio*, now practiced in our place, must acknowledge a few fundamental premises if it is going to be truly effective. Our attitude must be such that we believe wholeheartedly that the God of creation and redemption can be encountered here, and that God's sustaining Spirit will give us the inspiration to utter faithfully the language we hear arising from the depths of the body. Also, we must affirm that this endeavor is integral to our original calling as tillers and keepers. But *faithfulness* to the discipline, a commitment to our practice that exceeds our need simply to have a backyard hobby, is of utmost importance, and this steadfastness extends not only to what we do but to the means by which we do it. We must go to great lengths to observe that in our practice we are always reading and ruminating on the true text of our place, on what it *is*, as opposed to what we want it to be. In so doing we will ensure that the voices we discern there are not simply those imposed by us in our haste to make our gardens grow. Our priority should therefore be a devotion to maintaining the integrity of our biotic community so that in our listening its distinctive tones can be heard with as few obstructions as possible. This is why gardening organically, accomplished without the aid of so many technological quick fixes, is essential.

Our work, however, must not conclude with *meditatio*; our response (*oratio*) to the God whom we meet is also vital, for the benefit of our community. Encountering persons in our midst through our tilling and keeping is, as Buber has suggested, less a technical science than a creative art. It is a task entered into faithfully in the hope that the Eternal You may be known and "actualized." This occurs in such a way that, though the other is "led across into the It-world" to be represented as object, it still carries with it the potential to be addressed as You.

Consequently, "the receptive beholder may be bodily confronted now and again."[12] Thus, the tiller and keeper will be concerned with the promotion of sustainable agriculture and the preservation of ecological integrity; moreover, he or she will also be calling forth meaning, personality, God's presence in *this* place. But there must be a careful consideration of the tools we use to facilitate this "bringing forth."

The means by which we do our tilling and keeping will be radically removed from the practices so commonly accepted today. As we saw in chapter 3, most modern farmers are too often prevented from recognizing the faces in their biotic communities because of their blind insistence on the importance of their complex technologies. These artifacts of the It-world only sever existing relationships between person and place and inhibit potential encounters between I and You, thus making any acknowledgment of the subtle language of the fields nearly impossible. The alternative community, by contrast, the body of Christ whose concern is ecological and spiritual liberation, will be recognized by its use of alternative technologies. Here the spears and other intrusive weapons of our aggressive culture must be effectively transformed into the pruning hooks of *shalom*. This will be a necessary first step in our move toward envisioning the practice of gardening as a new form of spiritual exercise.

Gardening as Spiritual Exercise

Those who have practiced *lectio divina* know that the most difficult obstacle to overcome in hearing the voice of God speaking through a scared text is the elimination of irritating distractions that can so easily send our minds wandering down one rabbit trail after another. Certainly finding the time in our busy schedules is a daunting enough task, but even when this has been accomplished, we know that our real work has only just begun. We must then attend to the clutter that surrounds us. Centuries ago, the Desert Fathers spoke disparagingly of the *logismoi* that intruded on their spiritual practice, those "trains of thought, strings of considerations, that invaded the heart, occluded it, divided it, and destroyed any chance of a single-hearted devotion to, search for, God."[13] In our human weakness, our attention can be drawn away from our ultimate goal by the most insignificant of diversions. And the same can be said of our practice of gardening as a spiritual discipline.

The tiller and keeper whose objective is to approach his or her place with the intent of "holy listening" must also be aware of a different kind of *logismoi* that can stand in the way. In a society mesmerized and obsessed with the allure of so many labor-saving devices, the temptation to replace our hope of genuine encounter with a desire for efficiency and impressive results is distracting indeed. When a concern for productivity overshadows our intent to be authentically engaged in the process of meaningful dialogue—that is, when we are more concerned with growing bigger and better tomatoes than learning the language of our fields—then our project is doomed from the start. Our interest is not in "buying time" but rather in "spending time" with our place, and this guiding principle will have its effect on the tools we use. The instruments that will best facilitate our creative interaction with our biotic community will not be the latest or the loudest toys on the market. Simplicity of means— becoming acquainted once again with the lowly shovel, rake, and hoe—is what best enables us to hear the still small voice of the Creator whispering through the lives of the human and non-human neighbors who meet us where we live and breathe and have our being.

Perhaps the most helpful distinction we can make with respect to the tools we use in our gardens is between devices that are "automated," on the one hand, and those that are "participatory," on the other. The latter, as Erazim Kohak has observed, will allow the meaning of a human act to stand out and permit the relationship between I and You to be perceived most clearly.[14] Automated tools, by contrast, only conceal the encounter behind the veil of so many intermediate links; they transform the You inevitably into an It. For example, one person may choose to purchase vegetables from her local supermarket—commodities that, on average, travel about 1,300 miles to make it to her kitchen—while another may commit to the year-long task of composting, tilling, sowing and harvesting her garden to provide similar nourishment for her body. For the latter, there will be nothing anonymous about the platter of sweet corn she places before her family in August or the pumpkin pie she serves for Thanksgiving in November. In constant dialogue with the soil and with her place, she may be, in Buber's words, "bodily confronted now and again" in everything she brings forth from the earth. When this occurs, "mutual actualization" can begin to take place; that is, God can be known distinctively in a place as You, and the I who encounters the divine can also be experienced not as a solitary ego, but as one who stands in relation, as one who is truly human.

It would seem that one of the main objectives in creating bigger and better machines, whether for the garden or for agricultural fields, is to provide an efficient means of food production that sidesteps the inconvenience of getting our hands messy, as if dirt beneath our fingernails were not just an embarrassing social faux pas but a certain sign of moral corruption. But one of the real joys of organic gardening and the holy listening that can accompany it is the opportunity to sink our hands into a rich soil that we have nurtured over the course of many seasons through the practice of composting. Many Americans, however, seem to have little interest in trying to replenish, in whatever small way, this vital gift of nature. Every summer residential streets are lined with trash bags and garbage bins filled with grass clippings and leaves, set out on the curbs to be hauled away to some more convenient location. What is overlooked in this all too common practice is the fact that with every container of organic refuse removed from our sight, a conversation is lost. If these materials were to remain with us to be cared for in a disciplined way, they could soon replenish the structure, minerals, and other nutrients that are now lacking in our neglected and abused soils. But composting has simply not captured the imaginations of the masses, and certainly only an eccentric few would regard the practice as a spiritual exercise.

The problem may lie in the perception that our soil is little more than an inert medium through which the chemicals necessary for plant growth are borne. This is what the science of agriculture seems to be telling us today as more and more energy is expended in the production of nitrogen, phosphorous, and potassium supplements so that we can continue to see "miracle growth" in our kitchen gardens. But the artist, the keeper of soils, knows that the rich earth out of which we were all fashioned is not simply some inert stuff through which our super chemicals pulse on their way to the roots of plants. Rather, our diverse soils, so distinctive in each bioregion across the planet, are very much alive, and as such they need our continuous attention and care. They are, as Wes Jackson notes, enormously complex ecosystems unto themselves:

> Soil is a placenta or matrix, a living organism which is larger than the life it supports, a tough elastic membrane which has given rise to many life forms and has watched the thousands of species from their first experiments at survival, many of them through millennia-long roaring successes and even dominion before their decline and demise.[15]

One can certainly get a sense of this complexity by simply scooping a handful of earth from well-tended land and observing its structure under a microscope. Far from being inert, this soil will be teaming with myriad forms of life, from bacteria, to fungal mycelia, to actinomycetes. Moving on up the evolutionary ladder, one will also find insects, insect larvae, nematodes, and earthworms (to name only a few). It would be instructive to compare this sample with one taken from the field of a farmer who practices the mechanized and chemicalized form of agriculture so prevalent today. The chances are very high that the biological activity in his or her soil would be quite minimal by contrast, and activity would certainly decline as it continued to be "set upon"[16] by so many forms of modern agricultural technology. And here we can note an irony: the soils most likely to reveal the face of the Eternal You—those that have the most ecological integrity, to use Leopold's term—will probably not be found in the agricultural fields that are now being farmed across the country. Rather, the rich "placenta" or "matrix" that Jackson extols is most likely to be discovered in your own backyard.

And right in your own backyard is where the spiritual practice of tilling and keeping can best begin. There is no better way to be introduced to the kind of discipline required by gardening organically than to commit to the practice, sustained over a year's time, of composting the carbonaceous and nitrogenous materials produced every day by your own household. Perhaps more than any other task in the garden, I have been most rewarded in my reading and ruminating on the "text" of my compost pile. There are parables to be learned here. Observing the process of decomposition over time challenges everything we seem to know about drawing so stark a contrast between the goodness of life and the tragedy of death. In the middle of winter, this mass of leaves, soil, manure, and old lawn clippings can produce internal temperatures as high as 140 degrees Fahrenheit, enough to melt any snow that might fall on it. Indeed, it is not uncommon to see stray or wild animals stretched out on top of the pile in the middle of the day, soaking up the sun from above and heat from below. And in all of this there is at least one inevitable question: Is this really just a mass of dead stuff, well on its way to "getting deader," or has this decomposition miraculously provided the conditions for new life? Of course the latter is the case, and quite obvious from a biological point of view. But how often has our religious sensibility been reconciled to this verity of nature? How often have we allowed death the satisfaction of final victory or permitted the grave to deliver its ultimate sting?

The Spirit certainly speaks as I listen carefully to my compost, and she assures me that in this life, and truly in our deaths, nothing is final. When it comes time to turn the pile—that is, when I need to mix things up to aerate it—I have gotten into the habit of repeating the words of the poet John Greenleaf Whittier, a little mantra following the dialogue I have enjoyed over the last several months:

> Night is the mother of the day, and winter of the spring,
> And ever upon old decay, the greenest mosses cling.

We do our best to reject this simple truth when it comes to preparing for our own deaths. We want to embalm our corpses and seal them in concrete vaults in an attempt to stave off the inevitable. But in so doing we deny ourselves the opportunity to acknowledge in our faith what Scripture has long told us about our ultimate destiny: from dust we came, and to dust we shall return. But if there is anything I have learned in my ruminations on the organic refuse of my life steaming in the cool of a spring morning, it is that arid and lifeless "dust" is not that from which we were made, nor is it that to which we will ultimately return. Rather, earth, with all its micro-organism, fungi, insects, and larvae, is our body's primal source, and I can only hope that it will be the home to which my body will one day return to nourish and support the human and nonhuman others who will follow me in my place.

This is no doubt the perspective behind the rising interest in "green burials" in both the United States and Europe. Many of us simply do not want to be denied our final participation in one of the great mysteries of life as the elements of our bodies are gradually taken up into the soil, grasses, and trees that surround our final resting places. There is in the enormity of this process, as Walt Whitman knew so well, an eternal wisdom to be learned:

> Now I am terrified at the earth, it is that calm and
> patient,
> It grows such sweet things out of such corruptions,
> It turns harmless and stainless on its axis, with such
> endless succession of diseased corpses,

It distills exquisite winds out of such infused fetor,
It renews with such unwitting looks its prodigal, annual,
    sumptuous crops,
It gives such divine materials to men, and accepts such
    leavings from them at last.[17]

Whitman's contemporary, Henry David Thoreau, was equally captivated—and perhaps even terrified—by the incomprehensible workings of the fields and forests that surrounded him in Concord, Massachusetts. Near the end of his life, his attention turned toward the auspicious beginnings that lay dormant in dead things, particularly seeds. His final manuscript, *The Dispersion of Seeds*, on which he continued to work right up until the time of his death, was in fact a response to a mistaken commonplace notion of his day that some plants could actually spring up spontaneously in nature. Thoreau was enough of a materialist to know that in his biotic community—which he observed with the faithfulness and tenacity of one on a spiritual quest—life could not be brought inexplicably into existence out of nothing. It was in fact seeds, disseminated through their ecological habitats by wind, water, birds, and mammals, that were responsible for the growth of the pitch pine, white birch, Canadian thistle, and scores of other woody and herbaceous species that he encountered in his place. Although he was able to demonstrate this truth of nature to the satisfaction of his intellectual curiosity, the paradox and mystery of his disciplined observations still remained: from an essentially dead object, and often in the harshest of circumstances, life can miraculously spring forth. His fascination with the complexity and beauty of nature could not be suppressed by the objectivity of his scientific conclusions, and toward the end of his life he was able to summarize the importance of his work in a kind of ecological credo: "Though I do not believe that a plant will spring up where no seed has been, I have great faith in a seed. . . . Convince me that you have a seed there, and I am prepared to expect wonders."[18]

"Convince me that you have a seed there." I have often kept

these words of Thoreau in mind as I have tilled the soil and prepared my garden beds for springtime sowing. With the increasing prominence of hybridized seeds in nearly every hardware and garden store across the country, and with what we now know about how some of these have been manipulated and reconfigured by seed company geneticists, it is a most relevant question to consider. Can you convince me that I have a seed here? Can I indeed expect wonders, as Jesus did from the mustard seed, or just so many "special effects"? But perhaps the most poignant question we can bring to our seeds every spring has to do with their potential for authentic dialogue and mutual actualization. What kind of stories can we hope to encounter here? Will we hear the voices of untold generations speaking from the past, or will we simply perceive the din of some faceless life-science lab where the bottom line is the bottom line? It is one of the overlooked tragedies of the past half century that so many heirloom varieties of vegetable plants, once so common in local biotic communities around the globe, have now all but disappeared.

Only fifty years ago, most farmers and kitchen gardeners participated in amateur selection work in order to improve their stock, saving seed from plants that seemed particularly well adapted to their habitat. In the 1980s, however, multinational companies began buying up small, family-owned seed companies and restricting their research to the production of F1 hybrids bred to grow commercially in the widest range of climates and habitats. As a result, thousands of heirloom varieties were simply ignored; many have now disappeared. And the trend continues.

As Sue Stickland has noted, the extent of lost biodiversity is alarming indeed:

In the US and Canada, two thirds of the nearly 5000 non-hybrid vegetable varieties that were offered in 1984 catalogs had been dropped by 1994. The situation is even worse in Europe, where substantial numbers of traditional varieties—often those adapted to local climates and cultures—which were available until two decades ago can no longer be obtained. For example, in France the 1925 seed list of the Vilmorin seed company offered more varieties of cabbage, beetroot, melons, and onions, than were available on the entire French seed market in the 1980s.[19]

Given these statistics it is easy to see how planting heirloom vegetables in the kitchen garden is as much a political statement as it is an act of faith. It offers a resounding "No!" to the disturbing trend toward biotic uniformity witnessed around the world in the last few decades. Thankfully, cooler heads have prevailed under these circumstances in the form of a small but very enthusiastic network of gardeners who comprise the Seed Savers Exchange. Organized in 1975 under the direction of Kent Whealy, this nonprofit group has been instrumental in preserving heirloom varieties of vegetable plants from around the world through its Heritage Farm in Decorah, Iowa, and through the efforts of gardeners who commit to the discipline of saving seeds and making them available to other members of the organization.[20]

The list that these tillers and keepers have been able to compile is quite extensive, but what makes their efforts unique is their commitment to preserving not only the seeds themselves but the stories that accompany them. These varietals are not the ones that will deliver all the desirable "special effects" that allow for an easy go of it in the garden; they have not been hybridized to be resistant to certain diseases or fungi. Indeed, they require the very care and attention that many of us in this fast food nation would like to avoid. But herein lies their true value. Heirloom varieties of plants are our partners in dialogue, our neighbors who enable us through our tilling and keeping to perceive the face of the Eternal You as it becomes manifest uniquely in our place.

Some of my most gratifying experiences while living and gardening in Grainger County, Tennessee, came in the form of conversations I had with my human neighbors, men and women who were kind enough to share their seeds with me. Actually, our seed swapping only provided the opportunity for our gardening stories to be told, the words of institution, as it were, that ensured the efficacy of the sacraments that we spread out on the table before us. Sometimes I would sit for hours on a family's front porch listening to tales of how a certain strain of pole bean came to this particular holler or how a striped plum tomato had been passed down faithfully from generation to generation. Appalachian people tend not to want to talk about themselves directly, but if one offers the opportunity for a larger narrative to be told—a story that establishes their blood and bones in the land, for instance—you can be assured of an evening filled with lively yarn spinning. I was always fascinated by the way seeds played such an important role in these stories, as if in these tiny "dead things" a world of miracles lay dormant, just waiting to be brought to life.

When I walked away from these conversations—often with four or five little envelopes of community heritage in my hands, and usually with a quart or two of canned peaches or tomatoes—I felt that I had been entrusted with a family treasure. I knew that the faces of these people, my benefactors, would remain with me for untold seasons to come, but only so long as I committed myself to tending carefully what would eventually grow in the soil that we both shared—and only so long as I told their stories. It would not take much to convince Thoreau that what I held in my hands on those occasions were indeed seeds from which I could expect wonders.

And wonders did abound, as I slowly weaned myself off the workhorse hybrids I had relied on most of my life. The heirlooms I sowed took time and patience, but it was in their careful tending that I was able to ask important questions about the integrity of my place. Reading the text of the land, and listening intently for the voice of the Spirit, I was initiated over time into the nuances of a unique language. In the first instance, I came to know the dialect of the plants who occupied not only my small garden but also the fields extending beyond it. In the woods just north of my growing space I was able to find wild edibles that would have certainly gone unnoticed had my attention not been so keenly focused on my backyard plot. Wild garlic growing in the bottomland near the creek, for example, offered me a clue as to the kind of soil and habitat my heirloom bulbs might enjoy. And the way that so many different species of plants grew together in the woods at the margins of my garden made me rethink my insistence on neatly tended rows of pole beans, corn, tomatoes, and other common crops. Companion planting—pairing certain varieties of vegetables together for mutual benefit—soon came to occupy my spiritual practice as I learned the tried and true methods and then began to experiment with some of my own.[21] In all of this I sought to remember the insistence of Wes Jackson and others that in our tilling and keeping we should keep ever before us the idea of "nature as measure." As I became more familiar with the sunup to sundown rhythms of my little corner of the bioregion, it became increasingly difficult for me to imagine myself as *not* a part of this landscape. In this local Great Society, every creature had his or her role to play, and mine, it seemed, was to fulfill my human calling by faithfully giving voice to my place.

Tending to the growth of various garden plants provides the best opportunity for the kind of *lectio* we considered earlier—the reading, ruminating, responding, and resting in the text of our place. After clearing away the distractions that can so easily rob us of any opportunity for genuine encounter, our attention can be directed to the dynamic growth processes of our plants and to their habits of interaction with each other. What we are reflecting on, we must remember, is an often overlooked metaphor for the body of Christ. Just as the many human members of the body have their stories to tell, so do the nonhuman others in our gardens reach out to us with their own life lessons. These, however, must be read and understood in the context of the divine narrative of reconciliation and emancipation.

Our reference to this overarching myth is what keeps the tiller and keeper—the man or woman fulfilling his or her human vocation in place—from being simply one more gardener abiding by the principles of ecological sustainability. As commendable as these are, they are not entirely sufficient for helping us to affirm that the value and meaning in our place is indeed an intimation of the Creator's personal presence there. We might also say that this is what separates the purely "spiritual" gardener from the one who considers himself to be "religious" as well. We come to the text of our biotic community with the expectation of encounter and with the hope that in the confluence of will and grace, discipline and freedom, tradition and innovation, we might gain insight into the Eternal You who speaks to us from the depths of our place. Tillers and keepers are not merely "recreationists" who have chosen gardening as one among many possible hobbies. Rather, we are "re-creationists," resting in the assurance that our tending to the body of Christ is the liberating work for which creation has been waiting with eager longing. We have been reborn into a new way of being in the world. We no longer turn a deaf ear to the language of the fields, but rather seek out its wisdom, even in our most common tasks.

Most of us, for example, enjoy growing tomatoes. They are perhaps the most familiar vegetable in the kitchen garden and the easiest to keep alive. I am particularly fond of Cherokee Purple tomatoes, an heirloom variety that grows well in the hills of east Tennessee. Certainly the heritage of this plant is of interest to me, but its personality—its smell, its growth habits, the authentic taste of its fruit—never ceases to stir up my imagination. I will admit that I often sit with these plants in the cool of the evening, watching and listening. I trace the growth of their vines and observe the setting of their buds. I watch the bees bounce from blossom to blossom until the sun no longer provides them adequate light for completing their tasks. Perhaps more than anything, I have been impressed with the hardiness of these plants. They have a very forgiving nature. A broken stem is rarely a cause for alarm; I can simply remove it, set it in water, and soon have a new plant ready to be returned to the earth. From brokenness comes abundance. Indeed, everything about these plants suggests an overwhelming lust for life, a yearning for vitality at all costs. Vines that happen to rest on the ground, for instance, will immediately send out roots, reaching down into the depths of the soil for the life-giving moisture to be found there. After ruminating on the life and lessons of these personalities occupying my garden space, I am compelled to affirm a truth that I would do well to make my own: their readiness to forgive is of a piece with their very evident lust for life. The two go hand-in-hand. And so it should be among all human members of the body of Christ.

While I have been fortunate to have had the time and space to garden organically, I am well aware that many of us in urban areas are limited in our access to land, and some simply do not have the time to devote to this spiritual exercise. There are, however, alternative and equally fulfilling ways to come to know the presence of the Eternal You in your biotic community. In recent years there has been a steadily increasing interest in Community Supported Agriculture (CSA) programs across the country. A CSA is a cooperative effort between farmers (usually organic) and people who desire to have fresh vegetables and fruits on their dinner tables during the local growing season. There are a number of advantages to this form of community. In the first instance, those who invest in a CSA know where their food comes from and how it is grown. They are able to ask questions of the farmer that would only evoke blank stares in the local supermarket. Does she grow organically? Does he promote biodiversity by using and preserving heirloom seeds? Can he tell their stories? What vegetables and fruits can be expected, and at what times of the year? Furthermore, families and individuals can barter with most growers. Oftentimes monthly subscription dues are reduced if one is willing to commit to a certain amount of time in the fields pulling weeds, pinching insect pests, watering, harvesting. This is especially appealing to parents who would like to introduce their small children to the experience of gardening on a less intensive scale. It also allows the young ones to make a very tangible connection between plant and plate. But more than anything, investing in Community Supported Agriculture is yet another way to offer a resounding "No" to the agricultural hegemony now being endured in nearly every part of the world. In this sense, eating locally is one of the most political activities that we can engage in on a daily basis.

Eating locally also makes a profound ecological statement. Apart from the fact that it eliminates the need to expend fossil fuels in transporting our food hundreds of miles every day, consuming local produce ties us directly to the cycle of the seasons. Our CSA will not provide us with strawberries in February, and this is how it should be. However, it will offer to us those delectable fruits, freshly plucked from the vine, during the months of May and June, leaving us to savor such pleasures that come but once a year. In this way, the CSA serves to reeducate us as to *when* we can expect certain foods to be featured on our dinner plate. It also helps us to suspect the means by which we are elsewhere provided with ripe and ready strawberries while the snow still flies. There is no better way to be rooted in the personality of one's place than to commit to the discipline of eating according to the seasons: to anticipate what the next cooler of veggies from the CSA is going to offer; to lament the passing of sweet corn in September while looking forward to the squash and sweet potatoes that will follow on its heels; to note the changes in colors, tastes, and smells of foods harvested from April through October, an experience that is simply lost in the overpackaged, overprocessed world in which we now live.[22]

Finally, participating in Community Supported Agriculture provides not only an opportunity to enjoy the abundance of the harvest but also the chance to share in the disappointment of a dry season when the crops fail for lack of rain. This is one truth that we would all do well to remember and to acknowledge before every meal: despite its apparent regularity and abundance on our supermarket shelves, food is indeed a precarious and therefore precious commodity.

In our local biotic communities we are called to be poets and makers, careful readers of the text before us: the soil, the so-called weeds, the earthworms, the bluebirds and rabbits, indeed, every aspect of the life-world in which we practice our human vocation. We ruminate (*meditatio*) on the voices we encounter and in so doing receive intimations of the Eternal You. But our responsibility does not stop here. It may be enough for some merely to rest contentedly in the spiritual presence of the one whose voice is heard speaking from the depths of all things, but as imagers of God we are called not only to be men and women who engender a relationship with our place through the work of our hands, but also creators, responding faithfully and in gratitude (*oratio*) to what God has revealed to us here and now.

We do not seek to "set upon" our place in order to fulfill our own needs and desires. Rather, we endeavor to be that point in creation at which art and local ecology are joined in unison so that the Eternal You may come to presence as a special kind of language. This response to the Divine encountered in our spiritual practice provides a means by which others in our community might also hear the good news of God's creative and redemptive activity in the world. In short, we are called to speak our stories—our own, God's, and those of our nonhuman neighbors—and this in various ways—through poetry, art, liturgies, and rituals. In so doing, the Spirit of our community, the body of Christ, can perpetually reveal God's presence. This is the fruit of the sustaining movement of God through the place where we live and move and have our being.

Making a Place

By now it should be evident that what I am proposing is a spirituality that acknowledges the presence of a Mysterious Other in the cosmos, and more specifically in our place, with whom we can have a personal and transformative encounter. Indeed, the memory of this meeting may be what keeps many of us sustained in body, mind, and spirit for years after the event. But too often in our culture this story remains simply one among a host of others, unconnected to any broader narrative or to the life experiences of others in our community. Despite its many flaws, both now and over the past two thousand years, the church has nevertheless provided a communal setting in which our personal stories and the divine narrative can be heard and celebrated together, at least in theory. Herbert Anderson and Edward Foley are correct in their assessment of the limited success with which this has been accomplished. While pastoral care has focused on the psychological experience of the individual, worship has emphasized the mystical dimension of God's work in the world, the result being a wide chasm stretching out between the two. Add to this the fact that the stories of our biotic community have simply been ignored, and it becomes painfully evident that the church, the risen body of Christ, still remains broken and wanting in its charge to be an effective witness for reconciliation and liberation in the world.

It would seem, then, that what is most needed now is an emphasis on a new kind of mission for the faithful. The body of Christ, the community of believers living in communion with their bioregion, is called to engage in the constructive task of *making a place* for the excluded others, both human and non-human, whom they encounter perpetually in their midst. As I have suggested above, this can be accomplished by listening carefully to the stories coming to us from the margins and the underside of our life-place and celebrating these in our worship and life together. Through the creative work of both our hearts and our hands we can begin to make the kind of place where the faithful can rest (*contemplatio*) in communion with those whose narratives have been spoken and actualized, and thus abide in the presence of the Eternal You.

Walk into any church today, especially those whose recent construction has paid little attention to the sacred arts, and it is very easy to see why many Christians are uninterested in, if not outwardly hostile toward, a concern for place as an integral aspect of their religious worldview. It certainly does not fit into the stories of personal salvation so commonly heard in the popular media. And little wonder—many of today's worship environments seem to be more intent on offering sanctuary from a tumultuous world outside than in providing a means for encountering the Eternal You through its many inhabitants. The story of Noah's ark comes to mind here: Christians are herded onto the sacred vessel every Sunday morning as a means for enduring the tempestuous seas that will confront them in the week ahead. Unfortunately this is not a recent phenomenon; the great Gothic cathedrals of Europe—Chartres, Notre Dame, Cologne—were equally as concerned to transport the baptized from the world of perdition into the heavenly kingdom. While stained-glass imagery enveloped the believer in the visual stories of the tradition (scenes depicting the birth of Christ, the flight into Egypt, Jesus' washing his disciples feet, the resurrection), rarely did this include an affirmation that the created world itself declares the glory of God or that one can perceive there the face of the Divine.

It is significant, and perhaps reflective of a relatively recent cosmological awareness on the part of many Americans, that one of the more prominent features of the National Cathedral in Washington, DC, is its "space window," an acknowledgment, it would seem, of God's presence in the outermost reaches of the universe. But the emphasis here is less on God's handiwork affirmed in the heavens than on the human accomplishment of sending men to the moon. The window itself contains a piece of basalt donated to the cathedral by the crew of Apollo 11, a very literal symbol of the kind of "setting upon" that is so pervasive in our society. When we survey the structures in which we worship on Sundays and throughout the week, it becomes evident that, in most cases, the places where we celebrate God's creative and redemptive presence in the world are more times than not diversions from, instead of immersions in, the vicissitudes of nature. Consequently, the stories of the nonhuman others whom we encounter there are silenced.

With this in mind, it is not untimely to suggest that one of the ways that our careful listening can "bring to presence," to reveal, the Eternal You today is through a new approach to church architecture, one in which the neighbors whom we meet in our "reading and ruminating" can join us, symbolically and actually, in our praise of the Creator. What better response to the presence of God in our midst than to design a worship environment in which we are perpetually reminded that we are not removed spiritually from our place but instead have a deep ontological connection to it?

An excellent example of this can be seen in Thorncrown Chapel, built during the 1980s in Eureka Springs, Arkansas. In designing this structure, architect E. Fay Jones, following the inspiration of his mentor, Frank Lloyd Wright, was intent on creating a sacred space that would effectively "bring the outside in."[23] Inspired by the light-filled Gothic chapel Sainte Chapelle, Jones utilized mostly native materials—pine, oak, flagstone—to construct a chapel that appears at first glance simply to rise up out of the landscape itself. The many vertical and diagonal interior trusses mirror the branches and boughs of the oaks and maples surrounding the building. The furnishings are minimal and thus do not detract from the experience of finding oneself deep in the midst of the forest. But the glass walls on all four sides of this structure are perhaps its most important feature, for they allow for the ever-changing play of light and shadows on the floors and ceiling throughout the day, an effect not without its theological significance. Standing in the midst of this chapel, one cannot help but be reminded of the Psalmist's intuition that "the hills sing together for joy at the presence of the LORD" (Ps. 98:8b-9). The overall feeling is that in this space there is no clear line marking the point where the walls begin and the forest ends. Thus, Thorncrown Chapel reflects in a very poetic way the unique spirit of its place; it is not set upon the landscape but an integral part of it. Worship here only offers the opportunity for further insight into what we have been suggesting throughout these pages, that who we are cannot be abstracted from where we are. Our stories—of God, of self, and those of our neighbors—must be told and heard together.

Another example of careful listening that has brought forth

the language of place can be found in the personal sacred space created by artist and art historian Deborah Haynes. In this instance her creative work lies much closer to the craft of organic gardening that we have been considering. On little more than an acre of land nestled in the midst of the Rocky Mountains in Jamestown, Colorado, Haynes has engaged in her own form of reading and ruminating, and to the faces she has encountered there she has offered her own unique response (*oratio*). Realizing that her bioregion has in the last century experienced the damaging "setting upon" so familiar to nearly every part of this continent—the destruction of wetlands, for example, at the hands of gold and silver miners—Haynes has been careful to listen intently to the narratives that have preceded her here. She is aware, for example, that the tragic pain of the Sand Creek Massacre of Arapaho Indians still echoes in these hills, and she is mindful of honoring this voice in her daily listening. On the bank of James Creek, which forms the outer edge of the property, she has planted medicinal herbs—valerian, bee balm, St. John's Wort, purple coneflower. Elsewhere she has cultivated wild volunteers like nettle, feverfew, and mullein. In all of this she has been careful not to introduce species that are ill-adapted to the dry Colorado climate; in other words, she has sought in all things to maintain the biological integrity of her place. But what is perhaps most intriguing about Haynes's project is the way her *lectio* and *meditatio* have given rise to her own very personal *oratio*.

Haynes spends a good deal of her day ruminating on the others who meet her where she lives and has her being. Around her place she has constructed a path of sandstone tiles, obtained from a local quarry, on which she daily engages in walking meditation. Much of her time is also spent in bringing the voices she encounters here to presence through her writing, drawing, and work with marble. The latter is perhaps what best distinguishes her distinctive style of *oratio*, because it very deliberately employs well-chosen words or phrases to reflect what is only intimated in the darkness of this landscape, below language. A four-sided column, for example, is mounted on sandstone and etched with the words "[THIS] Place," a visual reminder that both her mundane and creative work—her sweeping, watering, planting, digging, as well as her drawing and writing—occurs not in a vacuum but in response to where she is. In the gentle ripples of James Creek she has placed a marble slab etched simply with the word "water." Her hope is that this named element will reveal itself over time by smoothing over the rough contours of the chiseled stone. In all of this, Haynes's intention is to be engaged in a perpetual conversation with the neighbors with whom she shares her life-world and to bring these voices to presence in her own way:

> On one level, this place is where I live, where I read and write, draw and work in marble. On another level, however, *[THIS] Place* is a creative project about contemplative practice in a particular place, and about belonging and community. I am exploring the vagaries about living at a particular time and place, this *chronos* and *topos*, cultivating both my powers of perception and engaging the land, its history, and its present state.[24]

Haynes goes on to say that what she is seeking here is knowledge, but not the kind of information afforded us by our instrumental reason. On the contrary, it is a *gnosis*, in the original sense of the term: a spiritual knowing. What is significant here, however, is that this knowledge does not simply remain the mystical possession of a single individual; instead, it is brought to presence through creative action so that others in the community might experience a similar intimation of the Eternal You in this place. Haynes's *oratio* allows for the *contemplatio*, the resting in God's presence, of others who share her life-world.

A final example of an individual who endeavors in all things to reflect the spirit of his place is poet, essayist, and farmer Wendell Berry. Perhaps more than any other author in the American landscape, Berry has provided a critical and eloquent voice for those who have lived with an abiding sense of loss and a yearning to dwell with integrity in their chosen places. Like Haynes, he is in constant conversation with the human and nonhuman others who dwell in his biotic community, a small family farm in Port Royal, Kentucky. The quote cited earlier perhaps best summarizes his perspective on the human vocation, especially with respect to the rising enthusiasm expressed for "global thinking": "If you want to *see* where you are you will have to get out of your spaceship, out of your car, off your horse, and walk over the ground."[25] It would be a mistake, however, to regard Berry as just another nature writer or Romantic poet, someone keeping alive the tradition of Coleridge or Wordsworth, for example. To suggest as much is to disregard the profoundly prophetic dimension of his work. Indeed, his classic text on the rise of industrial agriculture in the United States, *The Unsettling of America*, can be compared in many ways to the voices of the great Hebrew prophets Amos or Micah, imploring the nation to consider what the Lord requires: "to do justice, love mercy, and to walk humbly with your God" (Mic. 6:8).

Berry's literary work needs to be seen as a kind of corrective to the tendency on the part of many these days to fall into mythic mode when considering their relationship with creation. Berry is a "parabler" who effectively upsets our Walt Disney illusions about how nature works and where humans fit into the scheme. His is an insight that takes solace in "the peace of wild things" and emphasizes, instead of overlooking, the tragedies that have befallen so many aspects of his life-world. He engages the wounds of "an old tree growing," for instance, a sycamore that shares the place that is his own:

> Fences have been tied to it, nails driven in it,
> hacks and whittles cut in it, the lightning has burned it.
> There is no year it has flourished in
> that has not harmed it. There is a hollow in it
> that is its death, though its living brims whitely
> at the lip of the darkness and flows outward.[26]

Whereas a poet like Robert Frost might be content merely to reflect on the sublime beauty of the tree before him, or might want to consider climbing its branches to swing down from heaven above, Berry is not afraid to take the extra step and look within, into the darkness. What is inspiring is the fact that, though he may in no way be considered an optimist, he is nevertheless hopeful of what he encounters there, and this places him squarely within the tradition of the Hebrew prophets of old.

Over the past several decades Berry's parabolic work has been best represented by the poetic reflections of his alter ego, "the Mad Farmer." To many, this man is a fool, because he so readily eschews the love of quick profit or a preoccupation with his annual raise. He is not afraid to know his neighbors, and he does not fear death. Indeed, he stands for much that so many Americans claim to hold dear, despite the fact that these values are rarely found in our day-to-day existence. The Mad Farmer delights in his daily labor, whether plowing a field behind a team of Belgian horses or harvesting his tobacco crop with the help of his neighbors and friends. He loves his wife and family, he loves his community, and he loves his land, but not necessarily in this order. To his way of thinking there *is* no order; it is difficult at times even to distinguish these. Though educated, he is suspicious of higher education. He believes in God, though his abrasive contrariness makes some wonder:

When they said, "I know that my Redeemer liveth,"
I told them, "He's dead." And when they told me,
"God is dead," I answered, "He goes fishing every day
in the Kentucky River. I see him often."[27]

In everything he does he is wary of success, defined as it is by the powers that be. In his life, his desire is for nothing more and nothing less than peace and wholeness. The Mad Farmer is, in other words, the quintessential parabler: "As soon as the generals and politicos can predict the motion of your mind, lose it."

Wendell Berry has been exceedingly influential in persuading Americans to stop and take note of their cherished values and consumptive lifestyle. The reason he has been so effective is that, like Jesus himself, he knows how to upset the acceptable bounds of propriety, how to explode the world of our myths and shake us by the collar with his parables. He is a careful listener, an observer of his place. His *lectio* and *meditatio* are practiced with the yellow clay of the Port Royal countryside on his hands. His *oratio*—whether it be poetry, fiction, or essay—is in every way a faithful response to the voices he hears in his place. For those who know his creative work, it is not too much to say that it provides a sacred doorway to the Eternal You abiding in the hills, rocks, animals, birds, trees, and people of the Port Royal community. A quote from one of his early novels, *Nathan Coulter*, perhaps best describes the relationship that Berry has to his place, an ideal toward which we might all aspire:

> In a way the spring was like him, a part of his land; I couldn't divide the spring from the notch it had cut in the hill. Grandpa had owned his land and had worked on it and taken pride from it for so long that we knew him, and he knew himself, in the same way that we knew the spring. His life couldn't be divided from the days he spent at work in his fields. Daddy had told us that we didn't know what the country would look like without him at work in the middle of it; and that was as true of Grandpa as it was of Daddy. We wouldn't recognize the country when he was dead.[28]

In each of these examples, it is important to note that the creative work of these tillers and keepers is entered into apart from the community of the church. This is not to say that E. Fay Jones, Deborah Haynes, or Wendell Berry does not have an appreciation for the Christian faith, but their understanding of the tradition is no doubt tempered by a very healthy suspicion of what has gone on in the past. With this comes a need to challenge the narratives of the church, in good parabolic fashion, and this through the work of their hands and hearts. The result in each case is a new way of seeing the world, and especially a renewed sense of our ontological connection to the place in which we live. But their work also raises troubling questions for those of us who want to remain faithful to the Christian tradition and to work within it. Why has this kind of *lectio divina* been absent, or at least underemphasized, in the church, almost from the very beginning of its existence? How do we begin to change hearts and minds so that we can affirm our nonhuman neighbors as integral to who we are and thus as important to our religious community? Perhaps most important, are there any small steps that can be taken as initial overtures to the wealth of changes that need to occur with respect to how we perceive the value of our place?

The answer to all these questions, I believe, lies in the telling of our stories through the observance of new rituals in the life of the body of Christ. As Anderson and Foley have noted, given the peculiar nature of each worshiping community (and I would add here, each biotic community), our rituals will not be celebrated in the same manner in all places and all times, but each of these will nevertheless represent the confluence of the divine and human narratives, as well as the stories of our neighbors with whom we share our life-world. In the conclusion that follows, I would like briefly to consider one such ritual that has the potential for being developed in unique ways in church communities across the world: "homecoming."

Homecoming

In the first few decades of the early church, the body of Christ was nearly rent in two by varying interpretations of Jesus' life and teaching. While some, like Peter and James, emphasized a continuation of the Jewish tradition and implored those in their communities to remain true to the ways of their ancestors, others—specifically Paul—were intent on ensuring that Jesus' life, death, and resurrection would be interpreted in an entirely new way. In the course of the discussions the question of observing traditional feast days eventually came to the fore. Were the Jewish followers of Jesus still required to make their pilgrimage to Jerusalem every year, on Passover or during one of the other special observances? It is not coincidental that in those early years the festivals that had been celebrated by Jews for centuries came to be replaced with distinctively Christian alternatives. Instead of observing Passover as a commemoration of Hebrew liberation from Egypt—a feast that coincided with the beginning of the grain harvest in Palestine—followers of Christ came to celebrate Easter, an affirmation of Jesus' conquest over the tyranny of death. Similarly, whereas Jews regarded Pentecost, or the Feast of Weeks, as a memorial to the giving of the Law on Mount Sinai—a celebration that also coincided with the end of the grain harvest—Christians came to observe this day by reflecting on the advent of a new law introduced by the Holy Spirit. Now, through God's gracious bestowal of other languages on the body of believers, God's covenant—established with both Jews and Gentiles—could be proclaimed to the ends of the earth.

It is interesting to note, however, that while the Jewish feast days of Passover and Pentecost were reinterpreted by the early church, one Jewish celebration, or a variation thereof, is conspicuous by its absence from the Christian calendar, and much to the detriment, I believe, of subsequent Christian history. In the first century, Sukkoth, the Festival of Booths, commemorated the forty years of wandering in the Sinai desert by the Hebrew people. Like the aforementioned holidays it also reflected the agricultural orientation of many Jews living near Jerusalem at the time. Indeed, it provided them the opportunity to thank God for the abundance of their final harvest and to beseech the Creator for a better year to come. Today, the observance of this feast is foreign to most Christians, but perhaps more than any other Jewish holiday, Sukkoth affirms God's continued presence in the land of which the Jews are a part. This is the God who

> bring[s] forth food from the earth,
>   and wine to gladden the human heart,
> oil to make the face shine,
>   and bread to strengthen the human heart.
>   (Ps. 104:14b-15)

An autumn festival celebrated shortly after Yom Kippur, Sukkoth features the ritual of building booths and decorating them with all manner of fruits and vegetables. Central to this observance is the command recorded in Leviticus 23:40, which is practiced as "waving the four species": the *lulav* or palm branch, myrtle twigs, willow twigs, and the *etrog*, a beautiful and aromatic citrus fruit.[1] Jews gather in their booths during the nine-day feast and recall the lives of their ancestors who endured their desert wanderings while camping precariously beneath the stars. Implicit in this also is the memory of how these structures were used as shelters in Israel as the people of God harvested their fruits and vegetables. The festival is recognized as one of the great and joyous times of the year, when families gather, tell stories, and enjoy the abundance of the land in gratitude to God. Whether celebrated on a kibbutz in the Holy Land or on the balcony of a high-rise apartment building in New York City, Sukkoth affirms in a very tangible way that God is present to the people through the work of God's hands, creation itself.

It is perhaps a testimony to the success of Paul's largely urban ministry that Sukkoth found no counterpart in the worship of the early Christian church. This is not to say, however, that the compulsion to celebrate God's sustaining Spirit has been absent from Christian civilization throughout the centuries. The very profound need to gather as community and affirm the good fortune of food on our tables and water on our land has found expression in local fairs, church potlucks, and especially the secular observance of Thanksgiving in the United States. But these, it seems, have always been ancillary to the *worship* that takes place in the official liturgies and rituals of the church. The Christian faith, I believe, has suffered considerably from this oversight, raising important questions. We need to address these questions in a creative way if we are ever going to bridge the gap between the human and divine narratives told in the context of worship and the stories of the nonhuman others who meet us in the holy listening practiced in our place: Why is there no Christian counterpart to, or simply an observance of, Sukkoth, reputed by some scholars to have been considered "the great Jewish festival" during the time of both the First and Second Temple?[2] What does this omission say about the Christian faith vis-à-vis the natural world? Are there ways in which we might create comparable ritual observances of the very real dependence that we as the body of Christ have on our biotic communities? How can we begin to include in our worship the stories of the nonhuman others who share our life-world?

I have begun to think about this issue in a preliminary way as a result of experiences I have had attending the "homecoming" celebrations of small churches in the Cumberland Mountains of eastern Kentucky and Tennessee. The origin of this observance is not entirely clear, but some have suggested that "dinner on the ground," as it is sometimes called, became a central feature of many local churches sometime in the 1930s. This was a time when economic hardships in the mountains—brought on in no small way by the mechanization of the coal mining industry—made migrations to such northern cities as Columbus, Cleveland, and Detroit an absolute necessity. Improved rural education was also a factor in this phenomenon; with increased labor skills, men and women were no longer tied to the land in the same way that generations before them had been. Though this upward mobility might appear to be a blessing, it was not welcomed as such among those who were left behind to scratch out a meager existence in the isolated hollers and hills. Loyalty to family and place was deeply ingrained in the lives of these mountain people, and by the middle of the twentieth century, they saw their treasured values slipping from their grasp.

It seems that about this time many of the small churches of the region began observing homecomings—that is, pilgrimages back home—if for only a day or two, so that the spirit of the wayfarers might be renewed and a connection with their place reaffirmed. To an outsider, this ritual may seem like little more than a church potluck, with the exception that everyone is eating outside, either under a specially constructed shelter or on a blanket spread over the ground. But there is more going on here than a community meal shared after worship. Indeed, the meal *is* worship, the culmination of the Spirit's creative movement through the body of believers in *this* place.

Services begin in the church itself, with about an hour of singing, usually from shape note hymnals, themselves a unique creation of the spirit of the hills. Sometimes a special gospel choir will be on hand for the event, offering up songs to God with the accompaniment of traditional mountain instruments:

guitar, banjo, dobro, and fiddle. There is a sermon, but this is by no means the main attraction of the day. On the contrary, this distinction is reserved for an ancient ritual practiced too infrequently, if at all, in so many of today's churches: a foot washing. Men gather on one side of the room, women on the other, and a bowl of water, drawn from a local spring, is passed down the line, each person taking his or her turn in tending symbolically to the needs of a neighbor. Fathers kneel before sons, mothers before daughters, and welcome lost lambs back into the fold. Few words are spoken, but throughout the experience there is a very palpable sense that the deeds of the faithful gathered in this place are purely reflective of the Christian ideal of hospitality. And the ritual has only begun.

With the conclusion of the foot washing, men and women, boys and girls, retire to an open-sided shelter in which casseroles, pies, fresh vegetables, spring water, and other local fare are placed before the guests. Most of these are recipes that have been handed down from generation to generation, and all are the deepest expression of the maker's love for his or her community. As the food is passed and the plates are filled, stories begin to be told, recollections of past events that most in attendance have heard at least a time or two. But entertainment is not the objective here; rather, it is an assurance that what has been experienced in these hills by the men and women who have spent their lives here will not be lost to the wheels of progress moving on apace in the cities to the north. Words are spoken, but stories are also presented sacramentally in the food placed before each guest.

It is no coincidence that homecomings usually take place toward the end of the summer, a time when local gardens are heavy with fruits and vegetables. Most of what is served in this ritual has been lovingly brought forth from the land itself; it reflects the very strength and vitality of this place. Heirloom tomatoes, for example, the seeds of which have been a family possession for generations, take the place of the generic cardboard hybrids so abundant in typical American supermarkets. Turkey craw pole beans, the seeds reputed to have been found in the gullet of a tom shot years ago in a particular holler, replace the bland and tasteless varieties found in most stores across the country. In all of this there is personality—a face—that is revealed in and through the creative act of the communal meal. Implicit also is the belief that not only have human relationships been affirmed over the course of the celebration, but ties to the land have been renewed as well. A homecoming has indeed taken place.

A seasonal communal meal is but one of the many rituals that may be adopted by the body of Christ as we seek to celebrate the confluence of the divine, human, and nonhuman stories that are heard in distinctive tones in our particular places. In contrast to the Eucharist—which has often been interpreted in individualistic terms as a believer's personal reconciliation with God—this intentional *agape* feast offers the opportunity for tillers and keepers to affirm their faith in the divine narrative and its importance in their lives. But it does more: for those who have been faithfully engaged in the careful reading of their place, it provides the context for their *oratio*, their response to God's presence, to be heard and experienced, whether this be through the food offered from their gardens or in the narratives shared of the Eternal You encountered in their personal *lectio* and *meditatio*. This is more than a potluck; like the Appalachian homecoming, this new ritual can and should be celebrated as a true extension of worship. Special liturgies might be created so that the meal can be interpreted fully in the context of the story of salvation ecology, but this is not an absolute necessity. A self-conscious acknowledgment that the stories related here offer personal insights into the sacred nature of one's place, where the sustaining breath of God can be felt in all its mystery, is quite enough. It must be affirmed that what we are experiencing in this special community observance is indeed an intimation of the peculiar language of *this* place.

The bringing to presence of the Eternal You in any place will inevitably establish an ethos—a spirit—that is altogether unique and must be kept alive through faithful reflection and creative action. This will be demonstrated not only in words but also in the work of our hearts and hands. Whereas many interpreters of the biblical tradition have emphasized Spirit as descending in a rush of mighty wind, allowing those present to "speak in tongues" (Acts 2), our new theological orientation requires that we must now affirm God's Spirit as rising up from the very body of Christ itself—that is, from our biotic community—and enabling us to "speak our place," to pass along the oral histories and other creations of our hearts that lend meaning to our lives here. Spirit, the element of transcendence experienced among all members of a community of reconciliation and emancipation, is the undefinable warmth that animates the face of our life-world. Our stories are the means by which the distinctive character of Christ in our midst is made known, revealing the unique personality that has arisen—and in their telling will continue to arise—in the place where we live.

But in all of this, it must be noted that there is an inherent danger in returning to a heartfelt reverence for our native soil, and this must be guarded against at all costs. As has happened so often in the past, when we become enamored of the notion that our place is indeed unique among all others in the world, we can also be easily convinced that only those whose blood and bones come from the elements here are truly qualified to give voice to the land. This was the tragic sentiment that contributed to the genocide of more than six million Jews and other "undesirables" in Nazi Germany and continues to fuel the fires of hatred in hot spots like Jerusalem and Belfast today. It is the implicit assumption that the stranger within my gates can never fully know the language of *my* fields.

In a lecture presented at the Seventeenth Annual Prairie Festival in 1995, historian Angus Wright raised a similar objection to Wes Jackson's enthusiasm for "becoming native to this place," and we would do well to heed his words. Though an attractive idea, Wright said, we must be wary of its allure all the same:

> While I believe in being native, I am a little afraid of the self-conscious project of becoming native. Any historian must be. For just as imperial conquest has been one of the

most ecologically and socially devastating forces in the world, so has the fanaticism of nativism been a powerfully destructive force. Like all love, the love of home may be a jealous love, paranoid, intolerant and violent; or it may be generous, tolerant and giving. There are few things more needed in this world than the love of place, but love can be blind, and we need to keep our eyes open.[3]

And what must we be seeking with open eyes? Wright went on to relate a very personal story that struck a chord in the hearts of those present. Growing up as a boy in Salina, Kansas, he could not help feeling that he was an outsider: in this small and rather closed Christian community he was raised a pagan by his mystic-pagan parents. Yet his family was able to find certain places of spiritual refuge, one being the company of a Jewish family, the Cushmans. Every year while his schoolmates were preparing for the celebration of Easter, he and his father and mother celebrated the Passover Seder with this family of "outsiders." Wright said that the one thing that impressed him most about this ritual meal was the practice of always leaving the door open, just a crack, regardless of the weather, and placing a filled glass of wine in front of an empty plate at the table. The hope, of course, was that the prophet Elijah would wander by and be welcomed into the household. Wright would try to envision what this man might look like: wild-eyed, bearded, dressed in ragged clothes. But he imagined other possibilities:

> a woman carrying a message of peace throughout America, or a survivor of a Nazi death camp, or one of [Jerry Cushman's] funny librarian friends full of dirty jokes, or an unemployed railway worker, or a poet, or a man who had just lost his farm. It wasn't hard to imagine these people—my parents were always inviting them in off the streets to share our home and meals throughout the year. For me, Salina was a place through which Elijahs traveled all the time, and we were to welcome them—it was part of the Cushmans' religion and part of ours too.[4]

And so it is in the Christian tradition, despite the fact that our history often does not bear this out. "Do not neglect to show hospitality to strangers," writes the author of the letter to the Hebrews, "for by doing that some have entertained angels without knowing it" (Heb. 13:2). Turning to the "genius of nature," as some would have us do, we find this also to be a general rule. The biotic community is never static but always in a state of flux, of evolution. Over time, Elijahs pass away while others are welcomed in, and if they are amenable to the language of the fields, they establish roots and "become native." Such is the Norway spruce that grows just outside my window, and such is the bluegrass of Wendell Berry's Kentucky. And so it must be with the body of Christ.

Historically, Americans have been great place seekers but rarely successful place dwellers. No doubt this longing has been informed by a Judeo-Christian mythology rich in wandering imagery: the Israelites in the desert of Sinai, the Jews by the waters of Babylon. But another tradition has always lingered just below the psychic surface of our collective memory, that of the "new Jerusalem," the city of peace rising up from the earth (Rev. 21:2), where the people dwell secure in the sight of God, where they sit, "every man under his vine and under his fig tree, and none shall make them afraid" (Mic. 4:4). This is the legacy that must become the central focus of the stories we tell, the local narratives of our living in place. Homecoming, in other words, must now become the fundamental theme in those various and unique creations of spirit that allow us to see, if for but a fleeting moment, the ever-changing face of the Eternal You in our midst.

Living in Place

Throughout these pages I have lamented the tragic consequences of a Christian theology that has taken too seriously the transcendence of God, almost to the exclusion of God's immanence in our world. Many in our society have intuited this shortcoming of the tradition and have responded, somewhat dramatically, by seeking out new and appealing ways to affirm the movement of God's spirit in nature, usually by adopting spiritual traditions whose worldview is entirely inconsistent with the lives we live each day. It has been my intention in this book to show that, though the church has done much throughout its history to perpetuate division and strife instead of peace and wholeness, it is nevertheless *our* tradition. If we are honest with ourselves, we will have to admit that the Judeo-Christian paradigm is not as easy to cast off as some would have us believe. However, good tillers and keepers know the value of separating the wheat from the chaff, of saving seeds that are likely to bear good fruit and setting aside those that will not.

Perhaps the most significant theological movement of the twentieth century, liberation theology (in its various forms), teaches us to bring our heads out of the clouds of intellect and get our hands dirty in our local communities, living and worshiping with those most in need of the good news of the gospel. However, it has been precisely our intellect—our insistence on instrumental reason and the objectification of the world around us—that has kept us from recognizing the fact that our nonhuman neighbors are also in need of hearing the good news, of experiencing the hope of liberation and reconciliation. Thus, the soils of our tradition need to be turned, and new seeds need to be sown, but from stock that we have inherited from our predecessors.

In short, our affirmation of God's Trinitarian nature, the image in which we as human beings were created, must now include a recognition of the Creator's personal presence in the natural world, the Redeemer's concern that all members of the body experience true liberation, and the Spirit's movement in our biotic community that helps to sustain the peculiar character of our place. More than this, our theological anthropology—our view of the human-divine relationship—must also reflect this turn toward relationality, so that our understanding of our human vocation will not be so readily abstracted from the places in which we live. We are called to reflect the very nature of God in our tilling and keeping and to be engaged in the spiritual discipline of "holy reading" not just in our gardens but in our churches and other human and nonhuman communities. Indeed, as God is Creator-Redeemer-Sustainer, so are we also called to be cocreators working in faithful dialogue to reveal the Eternal You. But this involves discipline, not merely some vague emotion about what it means to be "spiritual but not religious."

As Flannery O'Connor knew so well, revealing the sacred in our midst requires time, patience, listening, praying, and creativity, all those qualities that characterize the work of tillers and keepers:

> An identity is not to be found on the surface; it is not accessible to the poll-taker; it is not something that *can* become a cliché. It is not made from the mean average or the typical, but from the hidden and often the most extreme. It is not made from what passes, but from those qualities that endure, regardless of what passes, because they are related to truth. It lies very deep. In its entirety it is known only to God, but of those who look for it, none gets so close as the artist.[5]

So we clear away the debris of so many former seasons and resist the allure of what, in the end, is only average, of what lies on the surface. We avoid giving in to the great lie that it is only the "spiritual" person who can heed the call to dig deep and approach the inaccessible wisdom of God. Like most artists, we live and work, hope and pray, eat and worship, with dirt on our hands, and we count it as part and parcel of both our spirituality *and* our religion. It is a mark of our vocation, our calling to approach what is hidden and to reveal it through our tilling and keeping, so that we, and all who share our place, might come to know the language of our fields.

Notes

Introduction: Going Home

1. Henry David Thoreau, journal entry, 20 November 1857, *The Heart of Thoreau's Journals*, ed. Odell Shepard (New York: Dover Publications, 1961), 190. See also *Henry David Thoreau, Faith in a Seed: The Dispersion of Seeds and Other Late Natural History Writings*, ed. Bradley Dean (Washington, DC: Island Press, 1993), 174.

2. In what follows I will employ the terms "Native American," "Indian," and "indigenous cultures/peoples" somewhat reluctantly, realizing that these are names that have been attributed to the First Nations of this continent by "the victors" who have been privileged to write its history. I recognize that it is a gross oversimplification to suggest that all Native cultures acknowledge and worship the sacred in the same way—thus, my frustration with the concept of "Native American spirituality." Therefore, when specific cultures and practices are referenced in this text—those of the Cherokee or the Zuni, for example—I will acknowledge the group specifically by name and emphasize their unique perspective. However, in some cases, it will be necessary to employ arguments that will require a general comparison of European and indigenous mythologies and practices—for

example, in drawing a contrast between an instrumental and an animistic worldview. In these instances I will rely on designations that have been employed by both Anglo and Native American authors when writing on the subject, assuming no specific nuance in the choice of the term "Indian" over "Native American." In every case, these words are chosen simply to alleviate the redundancy of employing one designation consistently throughout the text. For a helpful commentary on indigenous cultures and the problem of naming, see John A. Grim, "Cultural Identity, Authenticity, and Community Survival: The Politics of Recognition in the Study of Native American Religions," *American Indian Quarterly* 20, no. 3 (Summer 1996): 353–76.

3. Throughout this text I would like to emphasize the moral failure of our faith by referring to such tragedies as depleted topsoil, contaminated rivers, destroyed biodiversity, etc., as "embarrassments." Authors have been prone in the past to speak about these issues as "problems" or "crises," suggesting that these can somehow be amended with the right intellectual know-how. Using such terms, however, as I will suggest in the pages that follow, is more a source of the problem than a potential solution. Addressing our moral failures with respect to our "place," the bioregion in which we live, will require much more than simply a new intellectual approach to "the problem"; it will require a *metanoia*, a conversion, of body, mind, and spirit, in both the individual and the worshiping community.

4. In what follows, I am greatly indebted to the work of Wes Jackson's *Becoming Native to This Place* (Lexington: University of Kentucky Press, 1993), in which he makes this very claim, and to the inspirational work of poet, novelist, and essayist Wendell Berry.

Chapter One: Spiritual, But Not Religious

1. Charles Taylor, *The Ethics of Authenticity* (Cambridge, MA: Harvard University Press, 1992 [1991]), 14. Taylor treats this subject much more rigorously in his book *Sources of the Self:*

The Making of the Modern Identity (Cambridge, MA: Harvard University Press, 1989).

2. Donald Rothberg, "The Crisis of Modernity and the Emergence of Socially Engaged Spirituality," *ReVision* 15, no. 3 (Winter 1993): 106.

3. Ralph W. Estes has very effectively challenged the assumption that the "economic efficiency paradigm" is the best possible means for making good business decisions. See his *Tyranny of the Bottom Line: Why Corporations Make Good People Do Bad Things* (San Francisco: Berrett-Koehler Publishers, 1996). For a first-hand account of lives "narrowed and flattened" by corporate insensitivity to workers' welfare, see Fran Ansley, "The Gulf of Mexico, the Academy, and Me: Hazards of Boundary Crossing," *Soundings: An Interdisciplinary Journal* 78, no. 1 (Spring 1995): 68–104.

4. This is only a more empirically oriented version of what Ernest Becker refers to as the "existential paradox": individuality within finitude.

> Man has a symbolic identity that brings him sharply out of nature. He is a symbolic self, a creature with a name, a life history. He is a creator with a mind that soars out to speculate about atoms and infinity, who can place himself imaginatively at a point in space and contemplate bemusedly his own planet. . . . Yet, at the same time, . . . man is a worm and food for worms. (Ernest Becker, *The Denial of Death* [New York: Free Press, 1973], 12)

Finitude, for our purposes, is made all the more poignant not by death itself but by instrumental reason, which serves to objectify the world and separate humanity from it—a conceptual death, especially when the tools of this objectification are turned back on the human subject and his or her individuality is destroyed.

5. Alexis de Tocqueville, *De la Démocratie en Amérique* (Paris: Garnier-Flammarion, 1981), 2:385; as quoted by Taylor, *The Ethics of Authenticity*, 9. Tocqueville's reflections on American

democracy are revisited by Robert N. Bellah and his coauthors in their book *Habits of the Heart: Individuals and Commitment in American Life* (Berkeley: University of California Press, 1985), and shown to be exceedingly prescient.

6. David N. Elkins, *Beyond Religion: Eight Alternative Paths to the Sacred* (Wheaton, IL: Quest Books, 1998), 5. To Elkins's credit, he offers his readers a preliminary definition of terms like "spirituality," "sacred," and "soul," something that many authors writing on matters "spiritual" do not do.

7. Benedict of Nursia, *The Rule of St. Benedict*, ed. Timothy Fry, O.S.B. (New York: Vintage Books, 1981), 16.

8. Max Weber, *The Protestant Ethic and the Spirit of Capitalism*, trans. Talcott Parsons (New York: Charles Scribner's Sons, 1958).

9. For a very engaging personal account of a Protestant who discovers a unique sense of spirituality after spending several months in a Benedictine monastery, see Kathleen Norris, *The Cloister Walk* (New York: Riverhead Books, 1996).

10. This definition, and those for "community" and "sustainability" that follow, is adapted from the mission statement of Narrow Ridge Earth Literacy Center in Grainger County, Tennessee, where I have been fortunate enough to engage in the spiritual exercise of organic gardening over the past ten years (see www.narrowridge.org). In referring to the "mysterious Other" or the "Eternal You" I recognize that metaphors must always be employed due to her/his/its ineffable character. In the Christian tradition, this has taken the form in recent years of recognizing that God can and should be referred to as both "he" and "she," for any talk about an incomprehensible God will always be metaphorical, that is, will always have both an "is" and "is not" quality (see Sallie McFague, *Metaphorical Theology: Models of God in Religious Language* [Philadelphia: Fortress Press, 1982] and *Models of God: Theology for an Ecological, Nuclear Age* [Philadelphia: Fortress Press, 1987]). It is important that personal metaphors be incorporated in any description of this ultimate source because he/she is often experienced as personal, as capable of appealing to us as moral agents who share qualities similar to those of this most perfect Moral Agent.

11. Rothberg, "Crisis of Modernity," 105. Though I employ Rothberg's definition here, my conclusions about "religion" as a more specific term are contrary to his.

12. Wendell Berry, "Out of Your Car, Off Your Horse," in *Sex, Economy, Freedom and Community: Eight Essays* (New York: Pantheon Books, 1993), 19–20.

13. See Eyal Press and Jennifer Washburn, "The Kept University," *Atlantic Monthly* 285 (3): 39–54.

14. See especially Brian Swimme and Thomas Berry, *The Universe Story: From the Primordial Flaring Forth to the Ecozoic Era* (San Francisco: HarperSanFrancisco, 1992).

15. Gustavo Gutiérrez, *We Drink from Our Own Wells* (Maryknoll, NY: Orbis Books, 1983), 35–36.

16. Aldo Leopold, *A Sand County Almanac, and Sketches Here and There* (New York: Oxford University Press, 1966), esp. 219–21.

17. Emmanuel Levinas, *Totality and Infinity: An Essay in Exteriority*, trans. Alphonso Lingis (Pittsburgh: Duquesne University Press, 1969), 50.

18. Wes Jackson, *Becoming Native to This Place* (Lexington: University Press of Kentucky, 1995).

19. See Peter Singer, *Animal Liberation: A New Ethics for Our Treatment of Animals* (New York: Random House, 1975), esp. chapter 1; and Tom Regan, "The Case for Animal Rights," in Tom Regan and Peter Singer, eds., *Animal Rights and Human Obligations* (Englewood Cliffs, NJ: Prentice Hall, 1976).

20. Leopold, *Sand County Almanac*, ix.

21. For a more elaborate treatment of these two philosophical perspectives, see Peter S. Wenz, *Environmental Justice*, SUNY Series in Environmental Public Policy (Albany: State University of New York Press, 1988).

22. David Leeming and Jake Page, *The Mythology of Native North America* (Norman: University of Oklahoma Press, 1998), x. This sentiment is also the focus of a more recent book by J. Edward Chamberlin, *If This Is Your Land, Then Where Are Your Stories? Reimagining Home and Sacred Space* (Cleveland, OH: Pilgrim Press, 2003).

23. For a helpful discussion of how the Plains Indian came to be regarded as the archetype of all Native Americans, see John C. Ewers, "The Emergence of the Plains Indian as a Symbol of the North American Indian," in *Smithsonian Institution Annual Report, 1964* (Washington, DC: GPO, 1965), 531–44.

Chapter Two: Children of the Earth

1. This perception is brought home year after year, as throngs of Americans take to our national parks and court disaster by assuming that they are simply visiting some elaborate petting zoo. When a wild animal inevitably attacks and sometimes kills a tourist (as happened in the Great Smoky Mountains in May 2000), many are incredulous that such a tragedy could occur. Nature, for many who visit these wilderness areas, is perceived simply as a "consumer good," and when the commodity is "defective," they invariably seek out some form of restitution, usually the death of the "rogue beast." Such is the distance that has been placed between humans and the vicissitudes of nature.

2. See Philip J. Deloria, *Playing Indian*, Yale Historical Publications (New Haven, CT: Yale University Press, 1998), and David Hurst Thomas, *Skull Wars: Kennewick Man, Archaeology, and the Battle for Native American Identity* (New York: Basic Books, 2000), chapter 2.

3. Quoted by Rudolf Kaiser, "Chief Seattle's Speech(es): American Origins and European Reception," *Recovering the Word: Essays on Native American Literature*, ed. Brian Swann and Arnold Krupat (Berkeley: University of California Press, 1987), 525.

4. This attitude is summarized nicely by Earl Shorris in his book, *The Death of the Great Spirit: An Elegy for the American Indian* (New York: Simon and Schuster, 1971):

The progressive, historical man cannot enter the crystallized, immutable world of neolithic thought, for his very entrance into that world shatters it. The construction of that closed world in which everything is explained is so delicate that it can be hypothesized that the Indian culture was destroyed when the first white man arrived in the Western Hemisphere and demonstrated that he was not a god. (21)

5. Kaiser recovers at least four versions of Seattle's speech, each surfacing at a particular point in our nation's history. Seattle's original narrative, apart from being theologically insightful, is much more despairing of European culture and its religion:

> Your God loves your people and hates mine; he folds his strong arms lovingly around the white man and leads him as a father leads an infant son, but he has forsaken his red children; he makes your people wax strong every day, and soon they will fill the land; while our people are ebbing away like a fast-receding tide, that will never flow again. The white man's God cannot love his red children or he would protect them. . . .
>
> Your God seems to be partial. He came to the white man. We never saw him; never even heard his voice. He gave the white man laws but He had no word for his red children whose teeming millions filled this vast continent as the stars fill the firmament. No, we are two distinct races and must ever remain so. There is little in common between us. (quoted by Kaiser, "Chief Seattle's Speech(es)," 519–20)

One can get a sense of the liberty taken with this text when we compare the final lines quoted above with the conclusion drawn by Ted Perry's Seattle: "One thing we know. Our God is the same God. The earth is precious to Him. . . . We may be brothers after all. We shall see" (quoted by Kaiser, "Chief Seattle's Speech(es)," 530; from a film entitled *Home*, produced by the Southern Baptist Convention).

For other sources on this topic, see J. Baird Callicott, "American Indian Land Wisdom? Sorting Out the Issues," *Journal of Forestry* 33, no. 1 (January 1989): 35–42; and Albert Furtwangler, *Answering Chief Seattle* (Seattle: University of Washington Press, 1997).

6. Joseph Epes Brown, ed., *The Sacred Pipe: Black Elk's Account of the Seven Rites of the Oglala Sioux* (Norman: University of Oklahoma Press, 1953), 72. Of course, the classic text, *Black Elk Speaks*, as told to John G. Neihardt (Lincoln: University of Nebraska Press, 1961), has itself been scrutinized by scholars and found by some to be more a fabrication of Neihardt's poetic imagination than an authentic narrative of one Indian's nineteenth-century life on the Plains.

7. Shepard Krech III, *The Ecological Indian: Myth and History* (New York: W. W. Norton, 1999), 141. Equally as disruptive to the myth of the Plains Indian's complete reverence for the buffalo is *The Destruction of the Bison: An Environmental History, 1750-1920* (Cambridge: Cambridge University Press, 2000), in which Andrew C. Isenberg argues that the extinction of this species was a result of a variety of environmental and cultural factors, not least of which was the participation of Native Americans in the commercial trade of bison robes and meat.

8. Krech, *The Ecological Indian*, 134.

9. Ibid., 227.

10. In discussing Native American myths, rituals, and worldviews, it is often difficult to know what verb tense to employ. Speaking exclusively in the past suggests that the narratives of a particular tradition no longer play a vital role in the lives of those who still claim the tradition as their own. This is not a valid assumption. By contrast, using the present tense in discussions of native spirituality suggests that all Indians still hold fast to the worldview of their pre-nineteenth-century ancestors. This is certainly not the case. Add to this the general misconceptions perpetuated by Euro-Americans and others who wish to adopt as their own some semblance of "the Native American worldview" and it becomes very difficult to say anything of substance

without resorting incessantly to elaborate caveats and disclaimers. In what follows I will be employing the past tense when it is appropriate to context. This will usually involve discussions of nineteenth-century narratives and customs—for example, those regarding the hunting relationship between the Blackfeet and the bison, which are less relevant today to this cultural group. However, I will employ the present tense when speaking of the beliefs and rituals that still persist in a particular culture. But by proceeding in this way I do not want to suggest that *all* Cherokee, for instance, still acknowledge the importance of Selu, the Corn Mother, or that *all* Zuni still profess their faith in the emergence myth. But it does seem prudent to acknowledge the continuing vitality of these traditions in the lives of the people who still claim them as their own.

11. Joseph Epes Brown, *The Spiritual Legacy of the American Indian* (New York: Crossroad Publishing, 1982), 2.

12. Carolyn Merchant, *Ecological Revolutions: Nature, Gender and Science in New England* (Chapel Hill: University of North Carolina Press, 1989), 47–48.

13. Black Elk, *Black Elk Speaks*, 194–95.

14. Joseph Campbell, *The Hero with a Thousand Faces*, Bollingen Series 17 (Princeton, NJ: Princeton University Press, 1949), 3.

15. Alisdair MacIntyre, "Myth," in *The Encyclopedia of Philosophy*, ed. Paul Edwards (New York: Free Press, 1967), 5:434.

16. Joseph Campbell, with Bill Moyers, *The Power of Myth* (New York: Anchor Books, 1988), 38–39.

17. See Howard L. Harrod, *The Animals Came Dancing: Native American Sacred Ecology and Animal Kinship* (Tucson: University of Arizona Press, 2000).

18. George Dorsey, "The Arapaho Sundance," *Field Columbian Museum Anthropological Series* 4 (1903): 192. For a very helpful overview of the variations of this myth among Plains Indian cultures, see Harrod, *The Animals Came Dancing*, especially chapter 2.

19. Howard L. Harrod, *Renewing the World: Plains Indian*

Religion and Morality (Tucson: University of Arizona Press, 1987), 51.

20. Dorsey, "The Arapaho Sundance," 200.

21. Harrod, *Renewing the World*, 89.

22. Frank Hamilton Cushing, *The Mythic World of the Zuni*, ed. Barton Wright (Albuquerque: University of New Mexico Press, 1988), 5. For the Hopi variation on this emergence myth, see Harold Courlander, *The Fourth World of the Hopis* (New York: Crown Publishers, 1971), especially 17–43. An excellent video resource, *Hopi: Songs of the Fourth World*, makes it quite clear that, unlike some native groups, the Pueblo peoples in general have been highly successful in resisting assimilation into the dominant white culture. They continue to honor and preserve as much of their traditional heritage as possible.

23. M. Jane Young, "Women, Reproduction, and Religion in Western Puebloan Society," *Journal of American Folklore* 100, no. 398 (October–December, 1987): 438.

24. The Pueblo Indians of New Mexico and Arizona are comprised of a number of "social groups," each possessing its own unique myths and rituals. These include the Zuni, Hopi, Kerasan, Towa, Tewa, and Tiwa subcultures. Other groups in this region who share an emergence mythology are the Navajo and the Jicarilla Apache.

25. Merchant, *Ecological Revolutions*, 69.

26. See Gilbert L. Wilson, *Buffalo Bird Woman's Garden: Agriculture of the Hidatsa Indians*, Borealis Books (St. Paul: Minnesota Historical Society Press, 1987 [1917]).

27. Wilson reports that Buffalo Bird Woman was in fact averse to using manure to fortify the nutrients in her garden soil, seeing it as more trouble than it was worth. "We Hidatsas did not like to have the dung of animals in our fields," she told Wilson. "The horses we turned into our gardens in the fall dropped dung; and where they did so, we found little worms and insects. We also noted that where dung fell, many kinds of weeds grew up the next year" (ibid., 117).

28. R. Douglas Hurt, *Indian Agriculture in America: Prehistory to the Present* (Lawrence: University Press of Kansas, 1988), 38.

29. Gary Paul Nabhan, for example, reports that in 1910, fewer than 10,000 acres of Montana were planted in corn. After the introduction of Hidatsa and Mandan varieties to this state, the number increased dramatically, thus allowing the stark landscape to support a growing population. "By 1924, Montana's corn acreage had increased to 420,000 acres. In fifteen years' time, the three tribes' flint corns had allowed nearly a fifty-fold increase in Montana maize production" ("Harvest Time: Agricultural Change on the Northern Plains," in *Cultures of Habitat: On Nature, Culture, and Story* [Washington, DC: Counterpoint, 1998], 233). For an excellent resource on the history of corn in the Americas, see Betty Fussel, *The Story of Corn: The Myths and History, the Culture and Agriculture, the Art and Science of America's Quintessential Crop* (New York: North Point Press, 1992). For information on other Native American legacies, including the introduction of the potato, see Jack Weatherford, *Indian Givers: How the Indians of the Americas Transformed the World* (New York: Fawcett Columbine, 1988).

30. This particular narrative, of which there are several variations, is recorded by Sam D. Gill in *Native American Traditions: Sources and Interpretations* (Belmont, CA: Wadsworth Publishing, 1983), 132–37. For a less matricidal account, along with other stories about Selu and Kanati, see Marilou Awiakta, *Selu: Seeking the Corn Mother's Wisdom* (Golden, CO: Fulcrum Publishing, 1993), passim.

31. Carol Buchanan, *Brother Crow, Sister Corn: Traditional American Indian Gardening* (Berkeley: Ten Speed Press, 1997), 62–63.

32. Ernest Beaglehole, "Hopi Economic Life," *Yale University Publications in Anthropology* 15 (1937): 45–48, quoted in Gill, *Native American Traditions*, 140. Among Puebloan cultures, kachinas (katsina) are perceived variously as the spirits of ancestors recently departed, of those who died many generations ago, or those who never emerged as humans into this, the "fourth world." In this particular instance they are rain spirits portrayed by members of the Hopi kachina society, men who dress in elaborate costumes, including rather frightening masks, in order

to dance in the agricultural rituals of the village. In costume, the men believe that they actually become the kachina himself while at once retaining their human identity. The "smoking" referred to is sometimes called "smudging" today: purifying an area with the smoke of a special herb—sage, for instance—and beseeching the spirits to bring rain so that the crops might flourish.

33. Wilson, *Buffalo Bird*, 24. It is encouraging to see that in recent years similar provisions have been made among some gardeners with the "Plant a Row for the Hungry" program, where a certain portion of a gardener's harvest is marked for donation to a local relief organization.

34. Ibid., 27.

35. Buchanan, *Brother Crow*, 54. Marilou Awiakta also speaks about learning the stories of her Cherokee culture as a child on those occasions when she would help her grandfather plant corn in his garden. See *Selu: Seeking the Corn Mother's Wisdom*, 14–15.

36. Wilson, *Buffalo Bird*, 44.

Chapter Three: The Children of Abraham and the Conquest of Eden

1. William G. Doty, *Mythography: The Study of Myths and Rituals* (Tuscaloosa: University of Alabama Press, 1986), 25.

2. Bernhard W. Anderson, *Creation Versus Chaos: The Reinterpretation of Mythical Symbolism in the Bible* (Philadelphia: Fortress Press, 1987), 27.

3. In 1981 then–Secretary of the Interior and self-defined evangelical James Watt argued that the sale of public lands to oil and mineral companies should be of little concern since the return of Christ was surely imminent (see Colman McCarthy, "James Watt and the Puritan Ethic," *The Washington Post*, 14 May 1981, A12). For an interesting analysis of apocalyptic influences on former President Ronald Reagan, see Lawrence Jones, "Reagan's Religion," *Journal of American Culture* 8 (1985): 59–70; and Sara Diamond, *Spiritual Warfare: The Politics of the Christian Right* (Boston: South End Press, 1989).

4. In the mid-1980s, responding to the proliferation of nuclear weapons, Gordon Kaufman challenged the traditional conception of God's sovereignty, maintaining that it is *the* issue that theologians in a nuclear age must confront. See *Theology for a Nuclear Age* (Philadelphia: Westminster Press, 1985).

5. Lynn White Jr., "The Historical Roots of Our Ecological Crisis," in *Western Man and Environmental Ethics*, ed. Ian G. Barbour (Reading, MA: Addison-Wesley Publishing, 1973), 24.

6. Ibid., 25.

7. Wes Granberg-Michaelson, *A Worldly Spirituality: The Call to Take Care of the Earth* (San Francisco: Harper & Row, 1984), 60–64. This interpretation found favor early on among evangelical theologians hoping to rebut White's accusations. Humans, they suggested, are placed here by God to be "stewards" of the land. See, for example, the various essays published in Barbour, ed., *Western Man and Environmental Ethics*, and Loren Wilkinson, *Earthkeeping: Christian Stewardship of Natural Resources* (Grand Rapids, MI: William B. Eerdmans Publishing, 1980).

8. Augustine, *City of God*, Book 13, chapter 24, in *Fathers of the Church: Writings of St. Augustine*, ed. G. G. Walsh and G. Monahan (Washington, DC: Catholic University of America Press, 1952), 7:340.

9. Ibid., 341.

10. Ibid.

11. Thomas Aquinas, *Summa Theologiae: A Concise Translation*, ed. Timothy McDermott (Westminster, MD: Christian Classics, 1989), 144.

12. Donald Worster, "The Nature We Have Lost," in *The Wealth of Nature: Environmental History and the Ecological Imagination* (New York: Oxford University Press, 1993), 15.

13. William Cronon argues in *Changes in the Land: Indians, Colonists, and the Ecology of New England* (New York: Hill and Wang, 1983), 12, that

> [it] is tempting to believe that when the Europeans arrived
> in the New World they confronted Virgin Land, the Forest

Primeval, a wilderness which had existed for eons unin-
fluenced by human hands. Nothing could be further from
the truth. In Francis Jenning's telling phrase, the land was
less virgin that it was widowed. Indians had lived on the
continent for thousands of years, and had to a significant
extent modified the environment to their purposes. The
destruction of Indian communities in fact brought some
of the most important ecological changes which followed
the Europeans' arrival in America. The choice is not between two landscapes, one with and one without human
influence; it is between two human ways of living, two
ways of belonging to an ecosystem.

See also Carolyn Merchant, *Ecological Revolutions: Nature, Gender, and Science in New England* (Chapel Hill: University of
North Carolina Press, 1989), for a slightly different interpretation of the relationship between Indians and colonists. Merchant
argues that the ecological changes that Cronon records may
have occurred much more gradually than he leads his readers
to believe.

14. Cronon, *Changes in the Land*, 33.

15. Merchant, *Ecological Revolutions*, 58.

16. See, for example, Carlo Ginzberg, *The Night Battles:
Witchcraft and Agrarian Cults in the Sixteenth and Seventeenth Centuries*, trans. John and Anne Tedeschi (Baltimore: Johns Hopkins
University Press, 1983), for a historical analysis of this phenomenon in Europe.

17. Wendell Berry, *The Unsettling of America: Culture and Agriculture* (San Francisco: Sierra Club Books, 1977), 5.

18. Cronon, *Changes in the Land*, 74.

19. R. Douglas Hurt, *Indian Agriculture in America: Prehistory
to the Present* (Lawrence: University Press of Kansas, 1988), 152.

20. Donald Worster, *Dust Bowl: The Southern Plains in the
1930s* (New York: Oxford University Press, 1979), 81–82.

21. See William Cronon, *Nature's Metropolis: Chicago and the
Great West* (New York: W. W. Norton, 1991), especially chapter 3.

22. See for example Jefferson's *Notes on the State of Virginia* (New York: Harper & Row, 1964 [1861]), in which the author claims that "corruption of morals among the mass of cultivators is a phenomenon of which no age or nation can provide an example" (157). For further elaboration on Jefferson's glorification of the husbandman, see "Letter to the Marquis de Lafayette," in *The Life and Selected Writings of Thomas Jefferson*, ed. Adrienne Koch and William Peden (New York: Modern Library, 1944), 390.

23. The story of Agent Orange is certainly an example of this perverse beating of swords into plowshares. In *The Death of Ramón González: The Modern Agricultural Dilemma* (Austin: University of Texas Press, 1990), Angus Wright explains the curious connection between a wartime effort and a peacetime preoccupation:

> The powerful herbicide 2,4,5-T, later to become infamous as the main ingredient in Agent Orange, used to defoliate vast areas of Viet Nam, was first offered as an herbicide by Dow Chemical Company as a product of the company's war-time research. Farmers had gone into the first years of World War II with only a few pesticides available to them . . . known to be dangerous to people and to nature. By the end of the war, chemical companies were geared up with research and production capacity to offer the world's farmers a new array of chemicals to kill crop pests. Because the chemicals were relatively complex and/or new, very few people were prepared to question their safety or appropriateness in the field, and many were prepared to sing the praises of the chemicals because of their proven usefulness during and immediately after the war. Forty years after the end of the war, about one pound of synthetic pesticide for every person on earth is cast into the environment each year. (141)

24. Another development that should not be overlooked here is the simultaneous growth of the fast food industry, an equally efficient means for *distributing* the surfeit of food now

being coaxed out of the land. This would be another commodity to which the nation—especially its youth—would become addicted. For an excellent history and critique of this phenomenon, see Eric Schlosser, *Fast Food Nation: The Dark Side of the All-American Meal* (Boston: Houghton Mifflin, 2001). Equally informative is a more recent book by Greg Critser, *Fat Land: How Americans Became the Fattest People in the World* (Boston: Houghton Mifflin, 2003).

25. See Carson's very clear explanation of this phenomenon in chapter 3, "Elixirs of Death," *Silent Spring* (New York: Fawcett Crest, 1962), 24–43.

26. Osha Gray Davidson, *Broken Heartland: The Rise of America's Rural Ghetto* (New York: Anchor Books, 1990), 43. The research to which Davidson refers was conducted by Leon Burmeister et al., "Selected Cancer Mortality and Farm Practices in Iowa," *American Journal of Epidemiology* 118, no. 1 (July 1983), 72–77. Other studies conducted in the 1980s on the health hazards associated with agricultural chemicals in the United States include Kenneth Cantor, "Farming and Mortality from Non-Hodgkin's Lymphoma: A Case-Control Study," *International Journal of Cancer* 29 (1982): 239–47; Kenneth Cantor and Aaron Blair, "Farming and Mortality from Multiple Myeloma: A Case-Control Study with the Use of Death Certificates," *Journal of the National Cancer Institute* 72 (1984): 251–55; Molly Joel Coy, "The Health Effects of Agricultural Production: The Health of Agricultural Workers," *Journal of Public Health Policy* 6 (1985): 349–70; Deborah Fairchild, ed., *Groundwater Quality and Agricultural Practices* (Chelsea, MI: Lewis Publishers, 1987); Freshwater Foundation, *Pesticides and Groundwater: A Health Concern for the Midwest* (Navarre, MN: Freshwater Foundation, 1986).

27. In the last several years, a number of very helpful texts have been written on the subject of genetically modified foods. Perhaps the most helpful in terms of its accessibility and sophistication of scientific inquiry is Mark Lappé and Britt Bailey, *Against the Grain: Biotechnology and the Corporate Takeover of Your*

Food (Monroe, ME: Common Courage Press, 1998). Lappé and Bailey are Director and Research Associate, respectively, at the Center for Ethics and Toxics (CETOS), a nonprofit watchdog organization that keeps abreast of developments and applications of potentially toxic chemicals. Other resources include Luke Anderson, *Genetic Engineering, Food, and Our Environment* (White River Junction, VT: Chelsea Green Publishing, 1999); Jane Rissler and Margaret Mellon, *The Ecological Risks of Engineered Crops* (Cambridge, MA: MIT Press, 2000); Vandana Shiva, *Stolen Harvest: The Hijacking of the Global Food Supply* (Cambridge, MA: South End Press, 2000), and *Biopiracy: The Plunder of Nature and Knowledge* (Cambridge, MA: South End Press, 1997; and Martin Teitel and Kimberly Wilson, *Genetically Engineered Food: Changing the Nature of Nature* (Rochester, VT: Park Street Press, 1999). A Canadian organization that has been at the forefront of inquiry into farmers' rights and the corporate control of agriculture is the ETC (Erosion, Technology, and Concentration) Group, formerly Rural Advancement Foundation International (RAFI), whose Web site is a treasure trove of information on this topic. Their extensive publications are available at www.etcgroup.org.

28. This explains why chemical manufacturers have been buying up seed producers hand over fist in the last several years. See the ETC Group article "Seed Industry Consolidation: Who Owns Whom?" *Communiqué* 30 July 1998, 1–32, available at www.etcgroup.org. The extent to which major chemical companies now control the use of germ plasm in the hybridization and manipulation of seeds is alarming, especially when one considers that, in the future, we may not be able to purchase even the most common vegetable seeds without also buying a chemical application required for their germination and growth.

29. Marc Lappé and Britt Bailey of CETOS, for instance, cite tests showing that, "after being fed to test animals at high levels (hundreds of parts per million), glyphosate [Roundup's major ingredient] has been known to cause increases in bile acids, alkaline phosphatase and alanine aminotransferase, all of which

suggest toxicity to the liver and its detoxifying system" (*Against the Grain*, 54). Inert ingredients in the herbicide—like polyethyloxylated tallow amine surfactant, which allows for the free-flow of the herbicide through the applicator spray nozzle—have also been implicated in several human deaths in Japan and Taiwan. Thus, the authors conclude, these ingredients can hardly be considered "inert."

30. I can personally attest to this experience. In the summer of 2002, while living in rural Nebraska, I lost a portion of my heirloom corn crop to herbicide drift only days after seeing a local farmer applying Roundup in a field just upwind from my garden.

31. Lappe and Bailey, *Against the Grain*, 64. In a paper prepared in December of 2005, Sujatha Sankula, Gregory Marmon, and Edward Blumenthal reported that "[biotechnology-derived] borer-resistant corn was planted on 22.4 million acres in 2004. . . . This represents an adoption of 28 percent across the country" ("Biotechnology-Derived Crops Planted in 2004—Impacts on U.S. Agriculture," *National Center for Food and Agriculture Policy* [December 2005]: 64). The URL for a PDF of this report is available at http://www.ncfap.org/whatwedo/pdf/2004biotechimpacts.pdf.

32. Rural Advancement Foundation International, "Monsanto vs. Percy Schmeiser," *Geno-Types*, 2 April 2001, 2.

Chapter Four: Hearing Our Story Again in This Place

1. By the term "evangelical" I refer to those scholars who adhere firmly to what Edward Farley and Peter C. Hodgson have called "the scripture principle," the belief that the collection of writings in the Bible "contains a unique deposit of divine revelation—a deposit whose special qualities are due to its inspired origins, and which is to be handed down through the ages by an authoritative teaching tradition" ("Scripture and Tradition," in *Christian Theology: An Introduction to Its Traditions and Tasks*, ed. Peter C. Hodgson and Robert H. King [rev. ed.; Philadelphia: Fortress Press, 1985], 62).

2. Thomas Sieger Derr, *Ecology and Human Need* (Philadelphia: Westminster Press, 1975), 7; emphasis added. See also Derr's response to White's thesis, "Religion's Responsibility for the Ecological Crisis: An Argument Run Amok," in *Worldview* 18, no. 1 (January 1975): 39–45.

3. Derr, *Ecology and Human Need*, 23.

4. See, for example, Susan Powers Bratton, "Christian Ecotheology and the Old Testament," *Environmental Ethics* 6, no. 3 (Fall 1984): 195–209; Henlee H. Barnette, *The Church and the Ecological Crisis* (Grand Rapids, MI: William B. Eerdmans Publishing, 1972); André Dumas, "The Ecological Crisis and the Doctrine of Creation," *The Ecumenical Review* 27, no. 1 (January 1975): 24–35; Gabriel Fackre, "Ecology and Theology," *Religion and Life* 40 (Summer 1971): 210–24; Wesley Granberg-Michaelson, *A Worldly Spirituality: The Call to Take Care of the Earth* (San Francisco: Harper & Row, 1984), chapters 2–4; Loren Wilkinson, ed., *Earthkeeping: Christian Stewardship of Natural Resources* (Grand Rapids: William B. Eerdmans Publishing, 1980), especially chapter 13. A revised edition of the latter text was also published in 1991 as *Earthkeeping in the Nineties: Stewardship of Creation*, revised edition (Grand Rapids: William B. Eerdman's Publishing, 1991; reprinted 2003 by Wipf & Stock).

5. Biblical scholars have long recognized that Genesis in fact contains two creation narratives, each written at an especially important time in Israel's history. The Yahwist account (referred to simply as J, an abbreviation for the German spelling of "Yahweh") was written sometime around the reign of King Solomon (circa 950 BCE), known as Israel's golden age, and reflects a very pastoral understanding of God. The J account is found in Genesis 2:4b and verses following, and features the story of Adam and Eve. The Priestly Tradition (P), by contrast, was written sometime during or shortly after the Babylonian exile (circa 550 BCE) and features a more distant, powerful Creator. This narrative is found in Genesis 1:1—2:4a. When redactors arrived at a final version of the Pentateuch (perhaps in the fourth century BCE), they chose to place the Priestly version of creation prior to that of the

Yahwist narrative, despite the chronological discrepancy. The poetics of P must have seemed like a more appropriate choice for introducing the grandeur of Israel's God.

6. Wilkinson (et al.), "Who's in Charge?" in *Earthkeeping*, 209.

7. Lynn White Jr., "The Historical Roots of Our Ecological Crisis," in *Western Man and Environmental Ethics*, ed. Ian G. Barbour (Reading, MA: Addison-Wesley Publishing, 1973), 24.

8. Ibid., 25.

9. See note 6, above, for a brief discussion and definition of the P (Priestly) and J (Yahwist) narratives in Genesis.

10. That this image was already well established in the Christian/American psyche is affirmed by the fact that astronaut Bill Anders considered it appropriate to read aloud the creation account of Genesis 1 while gazing out of his Apollo 8 space capsule onto his distant planet (Christmas Eve, 1968).

11. When we consider the Babylonian context in which this account was conceived and written, it becomes much more understandable why the author(s) considered it necessary to portray Yahweh as a sovereign and transcendent creator. See Conrad Hyers, *The Meaning of Creation: Genesis and Modern Science* (Atlanta: John Knox Press, 1984), especially 50–56.

12. Karl Barth, *Church Dogmatics*, vol. 3, *The Doctrine of Creation*, part 2, ed. G. W. Bromiley and T. F. Torrance, trans. J. W. Edwards, O. Bussey, and Harold Knight (Edinburgh: T. & T. Clark, 1958), 185.

13. Pierre Leroy, S.J., "Teilhard de Chardin: The Man," in Teilhard de Chardin, *The Divine Milieu* (New York: Harper & Row, 1960), 21.

14. Teilhard, *The Divine Milieu*, 60.

15. For a fuller explication of Teilhard's thinking on this issue, see his short essay, "The Spirit of the Earth," in *Human Energy* (New York: Harper & Row, 1964), 19–47, or his much more elaborate work, *The Phenomenon of Man* (New York: Harper & Row, 1975).

16. Teilhard, "The Spirit of the Earth," 23, 28.

17. See Sallie McFague, *Models of God: Theology for an*

Ecological, Nuclear Age (Philadelphia: Fortress Press, 1987), in which McFague first introduces this metaphor, and *The Body of God: An Ecological Theology* (Minneapolis: Fortress Press, 1993), in which she elaborates on the idea.

18. See Teilhard de Chardin, "Sketch of a Personalistic Universe," in *Human Energy*, 53–92.

19. Stephen Jay Gould, *Full House: The Spread of Excellence from Plato to Darwin* (New York: Harmony Books, 1996), 4. Though this work deals primarily with cultural evolution, Gould has written elsewhere on the biological aspect of this theme, most notably in *Wonderful Life: The Burgess Shale and the Nature of History* (New York: W. W. Norton, 1989).

20. Nicholas Berdyaev would more than likely refer to Cain as a symbolic representative of the existential experience of hell.

> Unthinkable as a realm of objective being, hell exists in the subjective sphere and is a part of human experience. Hell, like heaven, is merely a symbol of man's spiritual life. The experience of hell means complete self-centeredness, inability to enter into objective being, self-absorption to which eternity is closed and nothing but bad infinity left. (*The Destiny of Man* [Westport, CT: Hyperion Press, 1986 (1954)], 268–69)

21. G. K. Chesterton, *Orthodoxy* (New York: Image Books, 1959), 80.

22. Walter Brueggemann, *The Land*, Overtures to Biblical Theology (Philadelphia: Fortress Press, 1976), 2.

23. Ibid.

24. Ibid., 15.

25. Ibid.

26. Ibid., 60.

Chapter Five: A Theology of Place

1. See Walden Bello, "Structural Adjustment Programs: 'Success' for Whom?" in *The Case Against the Global Economy: And*

For a Turn Toward the Local, ed. Jerry Mander and Edward Goldsmith (San Francisco: Sierra Club Books, 1996), 285–93.

2. Kirkpatrick Sale, "Principles of Bioregionalism," in Mander and Goldsmith, eds., *The Case Against the Global Economy,* 472. For a more detailed treatment of this subject, see two especially helpful books: Kirkpatrick Sale, *Dwellers in the Land: The Bioregional Vision* (Athens: University of Georgia Press, 2000), and Robert L. Thayer Jr., *Life-Place: Bioregional Thought and Practice* (Berkeley: University of California Press, 2003).

3. See Enrique Dussell, *Ethics and the Theology of Liberation* (Maryknoll, NY: Orbis Books, 1973), 151–59.

4. Gustavo Gutiérrez, *The Power of the Poor in History: Selected Writings,* trans. Robert R. Barr (Maryknoll, NY: Orbis Books, 1983), 44.

5. Gustavo Gutiérrez, *A Theology of Liberation: History, Politics, and Salvation,* trans. Sister Caridad Inda and John Eagleson (15th anniversary ed.; Maryknoll, NY: Orbis Books, 1988), 11.

6. Juan Luis Segundo, *The Liberation of Theology,* trans. John Drury (Maryknoll, NY: Orbis Books, 1976), 8.

7. Gutiérrez, *A Theology of Liberation,* 9.

8. Larry and Phyllis Scharper, eds., *The Gospel in Art by the Peasants of Solentiname* (Maryknoll, NY: Orbis Books, 1984).

9. Thomas Sieger Derr, *Ecology and Human Need* (Philadelphia: Westminster Press, 1975), 23.

10. For an excellent history of the Cumberland Mountains and their economic development at the hands of outside interests, see Harry Caudill, *Night Comes to the Cumberlands* (Kentucky: University of Kentucky Press, 1962). A more recent publication on the history and ecological health of this bioregion is John Nolt et al., *What Have We Done? The Foundation for Global Sustainability's State of the Bioregion Report for the Upper Tennessee Valley and the Southern Appalachian Mountains* (Washburn, TN: Earth Knows Publications, 1997).

11. Carolyn Merchant, *Ecological Revolutions: Nature, Gender,*

and Science in New England (Chapel Hill: University of North Carolina Press, 1989), 69.

12. Martin Buber, *I and Thou*, trans. Walter Kaufmann (New York: Charles Scribner's Sons, 1970), 53–54.

13. Ibid., 69.

14. Ibid., 55.

15. Ibid., 57.

16. Ibid., 150.

17. Ibid., 60–61; emphasis added.

18. C. K. Barrett, *The Epistle to the Romans* (New York: Harper & Row, 1957), 165.

19. Matthew Fox has written extensively about this often overlooked aspect of the Roman Catholic tradition, and with eloquent persuasion. See, for example, his book *Original Blessing: A Primer in Creation Spirituality* (Santa Fe: Bear & Company, 1983), as well as the more Christologically oriented *The Coming of the Cosmic Christ* (New York: Harper & Row, 1988). For a helpful introduction to the Greek Orthodox notion of sacramentalism, see Paulos Gregorios, *The Human Presence* (Geneva: World Council of Churches, 1978).

20. See, for example, Elisabeth Schüssler Fiorenza, *In Memory of Her: A Feminist Theological Reconstruction of Christian Origins* (New York: Crossroad Publishing, 1983), and *Bread Not Stone: The Challenge of Feminist Biblical Interpretation* (Boston: Beacon Press, 1984).

21. Mark C. Taylor, *Remembering Esperanza: A Cultural-Political Theology of North American Praxis* (Maryknoll, NY: Orbis Books, 1990), 169.

22. Ibid., 172.

23. Rita Nakashima Brock, *Journeys by Heart: A Christology of Erotic Power* (New York: Crossroad Publishing, 1988), 105–6.

24. Gerard Manley Hopkins, "As Kingfishers Catch Fire," in *Gerard Manley Hopkins*, ed. Catherine Phillips (Oxford Authors Series; Oxford: Oxford University Press, 1986), 129.

Chapter Six: Learning the Language of the Fields

1. John Dominic Crossan, *The Dark Interval: Towards a Theology of Story* (rev. ed.; Sonoma, CA: Polebridge Press, 1988), especially chapters 2 and 3.

2. See René Girard, *Violence and the Sacred* (Baltimore: Johns Hopkins University Press, 1977). For an introduction to Girard's often difficult work, two texts are particularly helpful: Gil Bailie, *Violence Unveiled: Humanity at the Crossroads* (New York: Crossroad Publishing, 1995), and Michael Kirwan, *Discovering Girard* (Boston: Cowley Publications, 2005).

3. L. M. Vail, *Heidegger and Ontological Difference* (University Park: Pennsylvania State University Press, 1972), 64, cited in Crossan, *The Dark Interval*, 40; emphasis in Crossan.

4. See Ronald Grimes, *Deeply Into the Bone: Re-Inventing Rites of Passage* (Berkeley: University of California Press, 2000), and *Marrying and Burying: Rites of Passage in a Man's Life* (Boulder, CO: Westview Press, 1995).

5. Herbert Anderson and Edward Foley, *Mighty Stories, Dangerous Rituals: Weaving Together the Human and the Divine* (San Francisco: Jossey-Bass, 1998), 37. I am grateful to Dr. Madeline Duntley for introducing me to this text and for our subsequent conversations about the book's importance for the church.

6. Ibid., 51–52.

7. Ibid., 44, referring to Robert J. Schreiter, *Constructing Local Theologies* (Maryknoll, NY: Orbis Books, 1985).

8. This discussion of the Holy Spirit has been greatly informed by the constructive work of Mark I. Wallace's recent book *Finding God in the Singing River: Christianity, Spirit, Nature* (Minneapolis: Fortress Press, 2005), where he argues persuasively that, in light of our present ecological problems, we must now begin to conceive of the Holy Spirit not only as feminine in gender but as the "green face of God." It is through the Spirit that God suffers with creation in its desecration at the hands of humans.

9. M. Basil Pennington, *Lectio Divina: Renewing the Ancient*

Practice of Praying the Scriptures (New York: Crossroad Publishing, 1998), 12–13. Two other helpful texts on this subject are Michael Casey's *Toward God: The Ancient Wisdom of Western Prayer* (Liguori, MO: Liguori/Triumph, 1996), and *Sacred Reading: The Ancient Art of Lectio Divina* (Liguori, MO: Liguori/Triumph, 1995).

10. Pennington, *Lectio Divina*, 13.

11. Ibid., 66.

12. Martin Buber, *I and Thou*, trans. Walter Kaufmann (New York: Charles Scribner's Sons, 1970), 61.

13. Andrew Louth, *The Wilderness of God* (Nashville: Abingdon Press, 1991), 61.

14. See Erazim Kohak, *The Embers and the Stars: A Philosophical Inquiry into the Moral Sense of Nature* (Chicago: University of Chicago Press, 1984), 170.

15. Wes Jackson, *New Roots for Agriculture* (new ed.; Lincoln: University of Nebraska Press, 1980), 10. For two very helpful "how to" texts on composting, see Stu Campbell, *Let It Rot! The Gardener's Guide to Composting* (rev. ed.; Pownal, VT: Storey Publishing, 1990), and Grace Gershuny, *Start with the Soil* (Emmaus, PA: Rodale Press, 1993).

16. I am borrowing this phrase from Martin Heidegger, who also distinguished two forms of technology. The first, *techne*, is a means of "bringing forth," that is, of working in harmony with nature to allow things to "come to presence" and reveal themselves as they truly are. By contrast, modern technology seeks to "set upon" (*stellt*), challenging nature to show itself only in certain forms (for example, as a standing reserve of resources for meeting human needs). See Martin Heidegger, "The Question Concerning Technology," in *The Question Concerning Technology and Other Essays*, trans. William Lovitt (New York: Harper Colophon Books, 1977), especially 14–17.

17. Walt Whitman, "This Compost," in *Leaves of Grass* ed. Harold W. Blodgett and Scully Bradley (New York: New York University Press, 1965), 369–70.

18. Henry David Thoreau, "The Succession of Forest Trees,"

in *Collected Essays and Poems* (Library of America 124; New York: Penguin Putnam, 2001), 442.

19. Sue Stickland, *Heirloom Vegetables: A Home Gardener's Guide to Finding and Growing Vegetables from the Past* (New York: Fireside Books, 1998), 59. For another excellent text that elaborates the cultural history of hundreds of varieties of heirloom vegetables, see William Woys Weaver, *Heirloom Vegetable Gardening: A Master Gardener's Guide to Planting, Seed Saving, and Cultural History* (New York: Henry Holt, 1997).

20. Lest anyone doubt that seed saving involves discipline and close attention to detail, Seed Savers Exchange has published a how-to text for the avid gardener interested in preserving more than seed stock for next year's planting. See Suzanne Ashworth, *Seed to Seed: Seed Saving Techniques for the Vegetable Gardener* (Decorah, IA: Seed Savers Publications, 1991).

21. A book I found to be extremely helpful in this endeavor was Louise Riotte's *Carrots Love Tomatoes: Secrets of Companion Planting for Successful Gardening* (Pownal, VT: Storey Communications, 1975).

22. See Mary Beth Lind and Cathleen Hockman-Wert, *Simply in Season: A Community Cookbook* (Scottdale, PA: Herald Press, 2005).

23. See Paul Heyer, *American Architecture: Ideas and Ideologies in the Late Twentieth Century* (New York: Van Nostrand Reinhold, 1993), 102–3.

24. Deborah Haynes, "The *Place* of Art," in *Arts, Theology, and the Church: New Intersections,* ed. Kimberly Vrudny and Wilson Yates (Cleveland, OH: Pilgrim Press, 2005), 171.

25. Wendell Berry, "Out of Your Car, Off Your Horse," in *Sex, Economy, Freedom and Community: Eight Essays* (New York: Pantheon Books, 1993), 20.

26. Wendell Berry, "The Sycamore," in *Collected Poems (1957–1982)* (San Francisco: North Point Press, 1984), 65.

27. Wendell Berry, "The Contrariness of the Mad Farmer," in *Collected Poems,* 121.

28. Wendell Berry, *Nathan Coulter* (San Francisco: North Point Press, 1985), 180.

Chapter Seven: Homecoming

1. For a fuller explanation on the history and meaning of Sukkoth, see Hayyim Schauss, *The Jewish Festivals: A Guide to Their History and Observance* (New York: Schocken Books, 1996), chapters 18–20. A more general introduction to Jewish holidays is offered by Stephen M. Wylen in his book *Settings of Silver: An Introduction to Judaism* (2nd ed.; New York: Paulist Press, 2000).

2. Schauss, *Jewish Festivals*, 170.

3. Angus Wright, "A Place for Elijah: Thoughts on Natives and Wanderers," *The Land Report* 54 (Fall 1995): 5.

4. Ibid., 5–6.

5. Flannery O'Connor, "The Regional Writer," in *Mystery and Manners: Occasional Prose*, ed. Sally and Robert Fitzgerald (New York: Farrar, Straus & Giroux, 1969), 58.

Recommended Resources

Action Group on Erosion, Technology, and Concentration

Readers interested in keeping up with recent developments in plant genetics and other biotechnologies need look no further than this website. Based in Canada, the ETC group (formerly Rural Advancement Foundation International) publishes periodic research reports and position papers on such topics as agriculture's growing reliance on genetically modified organisms, corporate control of the human food supply, the erosion of biodiversity across the planet, and new trends in nanotechnology. As they state on their Web page, "ETC group supports socially responsible developments of technologies useful to the poor and marginalized and it addresses international governance issues and corporate power" (http://www.etcgroup.org/about.asp).

Ashworth, Suzanne, and Kent Whealy. *Seed to Seed: Seed Saving and Growing Techniques for Vegetable Gardeners.* Second Edition. Decorah, IA: Seed Savers Exchange, 2002.

Even the first edition of this book is an invaluable resource for any gardener wanting to take the leap into propagating and saving heirloom seeds. Ashworth offers important instructions on how to avoid cross-pollination between varieties of the same species of plant, as well as helpful tips on harvesting, drying, and storing the seeds of over 160 nonhybrid varieties of vegetable crops.

Berry, Wendell. *The Unsettling of America: Culture and Agriculture*. San Francisco: Sierra Club, 1977.

This book has become a classic in the field of environmental history and agricultural ethics, reviewing as it does the rise of mechanized agriculture in the United States and its effects on the human spirit. Berry has been a prolific essayist, novelist, poet, and social critic for thirty years. He is known primarily for his agrarian perspective and his unwillingness to be pigeonholed into any political camp, liberal or conservative. He is an ardent proponent of Jeffersonian democracy and perhaps one of the most eloquent spokespeople for preserving the integrity of local communities. His agrarian essays have been collected and published by North Point Press: see *A Continuous Harmony* (1975), *The Gift of Good Land* (1981), and *Home Economics* (1987), among other titles.

Brown, David. *God and Enchantment of Place: Reclaiming Human Experience*. Oxford: Oxford University Press, 2004.

For those interested in pursuing the deeper theological implications of living with an awareness of the divine in one's place, Brown's book is an excellent place to begin. He suggests that if God is truly the generous creator whom the church affirms in its doctrine and creedal statements, then we should rightly expect that God can be found at work in all things, including the material world. He offers a highly sacramental view of both nature and such creations of the human heart as art, architecture, and even landscape design. This is not a light read, but it is well worth the effort.

Buchanan, Carol. *Brother Crow, Sister Corn: Traditional American Indian Gardening.* Berkeley, CA: Ten Speed Press, 1997.

Buchanan's book offers an excellent historical overview of traditional Native gardening as it was practiced among such cultural groups as the Cherokee, Hidatsa, Zuni, and Hopi. Though the book suffers a bit from a lack of footnotes and a very limited bibliography, it is nevertheless an excellent introduction to the myths, ceremonies, and gardening practices of these cultures. I have used this text with great success in designing an experiential curriculum for teaching children about Native gardens—in conjunction with Joseph Bruchac and Michael J. Caduto's books *Keepers of Life: Discovering Plants through Native American Stories and Earth Activities for Children* (Golden, CO: Fulcrum Publishing, 1997), and *Native American Gardening: Stories, Projects and Recipes for Families* (Golden, CO: Fulcrum Publishing, 1996).

Davidson, Osha Grey. *Broken Heartland: Rise of the Rural Ghetto.* Revised Edition. Iowa City, University of Iowa Press: 1996.

Davidson documents the decline of rural American communities during the farm crisis of the 1980s and investigates the root causes of farm foreclosures, chemical contamination of groundwater, and despair among residents of America's heartland. This is a very helpful book for anyone wanting to understand a major shift that took place in the sociological landscape of the American farming community just two decades ago.

Global Banquet: The Politics of Food. Maryknoll, NY. Maryknoll World Productions, 2001.

This video explores the politics of global food security, focusing particularly on how corporate entities now produce, finance, and distribute the majority of the world's food supply. It also features individuals and community organizations who are exploring alternative local means to growing and distributing their food. A discussion and study guide is also available. Contact Maryknoll World Productions, P.O. Box 308, Maryknoll, NY, 10545-0308; 800-227-8523; www.maryknollworld.org.

Harvest of Fear. Frontline/NOVA Special Presentation. Boston: WGBH Educational Foundation, 2001.

A two-hour documentary, *Harvest of Fear* introduces viewers to the complex ethical and social questions surrounding the genetic manipulation of our food. Through interviews with scientists, farmers, activists, and critics of biotechnology, the producers attempt to offer an objective assessment of the debate. Their success in this, however, remains a matter of opinion. Many have commented that Frontline did not take the biotech industry to task as aggressively as it could have.

Jackson, Wes. *Becoming Native to This Place.* Lexington: University of Kentucky Press, 1995.

Jackson asks what can be done to preserve the local traditions of small rural communities across America's heartland. Nearly a century ago, economically vibrant villages dotted the Great Plains landscape; today, most are little more than ghost towns complete with empty school buildings and vacant houses. Jackson suggests that this problem can be solved if a new breed of "homecomer" is willing to take on the creative work of becoming native to a particular place. This can only happen if one is ready to "dig in" to a local community, learn its history, and become committed to its vitality.

Jackson, Wes. *New Roots for Agriculture*. Revised Edition. Lincoln: University of Nebraska Press, 1985.

Jackson, a plant geneticist and founder of the Land Institute in Salina, Kansas, has dedicated his life's work to addressing the soil erosion and declining biological diversity he has witnessed on farms across the country and around the world. An outspoken critic of corporate agriculture, his research focuses on breeding herbaceous perennial food crops for supplementing the American diet. Grown in polycultures in a habitat similar to that of the prairie, these plants all but eliminate the need to assault the land on an annual basis through tillage and applications of chemicals. More information on Jackson's research is available at The Land Institute, 2440 E. Water Well Road, Salina, KS, 67401; 785-823-5376; http://www.landinstitute.org.

Jung, L. Shannon *Food for Life: The Spirituality and Ethics of Eating*. Minneapolis: Fortress Press, 2004.

Jung explores the role that food plays in the lives of Christians and considers the spiritual implications of how we grow, prepare, and share our food. He considers individual eating disorders like anorexia, bulimia, and obesity, but he also argues that our planet suffers from a global food disorder as well, which manifests itself most clearly in world hunger. He concludes by assessing the role the church might play in addressing these important issues. Jung continues his exploration of communal eating rituals in *Sharing Food: Christian Practices for Enjoyment* (Minneapolis: Fortress Press, 2006).

Leopold, Aldo. *A Sand County Almanac, and Sketches Here and There.* New York: Oxford University Press, 1987.

Considered by many to be the original environmentalist's manifesto, Leopold's *Sand County Almanac* challenges readers to think of themselves as plain members of their biotic community. This paradigm shift away from the inherited anthropocentric traditions of the West requires that people begin to nurture a new understanding of who they are and what role they play as participants in a complex web of ecological relationships. Two chapters, or "sketches," in this book are among the best-known ecological writing of the last sixty years: "Thinking Like a Mountain" and "The Land Ethic."

Lind, May Beth, and Cathleen Hockman-Wert. *Simply in Season: A World Community Cookbook.* Scottsdale, PA: Herald Press, 2005.

In the spirit of the best-selling *More-with-Less Cookbook* commissioned by the Mennonite Central Committee, Lind and Hockman-Wert have collected recipes and organized them according to the seasons in which fresh fruits and vegetables are most readily available. For anyone interested in adopting the spiritual practice of eating with the seasons, this book will be an excellent place to start. It also contains a very helpful guide that covers description, selection, storage and handling, preparation, and nutritional information for over fifty common fruits and vegetables.

Logsdon, Gene. *The Contrary Farmer's Invitation to Gardening.* White River Junction, VT: Chelsea Green Publishing, 1997.

Logsdon is a former editor of *Organic Gardening* magazine and works a thirty-two-acre farm in Upper Sandusky,

Ohio. His *Invitation to Gardening* is less a how-to manual than one man's reflections—often humorous and sometimes irreverent—on what it means to live in relationship with one's place and to take pleasure in its tilling and keeping. The title of his final chapter perhaps best summarizes his writing and gardening style: "The Aim Is Joy."

Nabhan, Gary Paul. *Enduring Seeds: Native American Agriculture and Wild Plant Conservation*. New York: North Point Press, 1989.

Nabhan, cofounder of Native Seeds/SEARCH, is an ethnobotanist and storyteller interested in the ways that past cultures interacted with and adapted to their local environments. He is a rare breed of scientist whose writing can easily slip back and forth between objective observation and spiritual insight. Two other books of interest are his *Cultures of Habitat: On Nature, Culture, and Story* (Washington, DC: Counterpoint, 1997), and (with Stephen Trimble) *The Geography of Childhood: Why Children Need Wild Places*, reprint edition (Boston: Beacon Press, 1995). Nabhan is also a seed saver, and many of the plants he writes about are propagated and offered to gardeners interested in keeping their stories alive. Contact: Native Seeds/SEARCH, 526 N. 4th Ave., Tucson, AZ, 85705-8450; 866-622-5561; http://www.nativeseeds.org for more information.

Petrini, Carlo. *Slow Food: The Case for Taste*. New York: Columbia University Press, 2001.

As founder of the International Slow Food Movement, Petrini is concerned to provide a genuine alternative to our nation's seeming infatuation with fast and easy, not to mention insipid, fare. Along with such notable culinary figures as Alice Walters and Deborah Madison, he reminds us that *real* food and local flavor can still be found in the most unusual places—whether around the corner or across the globe—if we only have the patience and will to find it. The Slow Food Movement is committed to safeguarding local economies and preserving indigenous foodways and thus provides a perfect complement to heirloom vegetable gardening. See also Carlo Petrini, ed., *Slow Food: Collected Thoughts on Taste, Tradition, and the Honest Pleasures of Food* (White River Junction, VT: Chelsea Green Publishing, 2001). For local chapters in the United States, contact Slow Food USA, P.O. Box 1737, New York, NY, 10021. The Slow Food website can be accessed at http://www.slowfood.com.

The Real Dirt on Farmer John. Produced and directed by Taggart Siegel. San Francisco: Independent Television Service, 2006.

This docudrama tells the story of farmer John Peterson's lifelong relationship with his family farm, from his early childhood years—detailed in his mother's 8-millimeter movies, shot during the 1950s—through the farm crisis of the 1980s, up to his present success as proprietor of Angelic Farms, an organic community supported agriculture (CSA) program. What makes this film so powerful is the knowledge that Peterson's struggles over the last fifty years have been endured time and again on family farms across the country. The success of his CSA, however, offers an alternative and hopeful vision for the future of American agriculture.

Seeds of Change

Located in Santa Fe, New Mexico, Seeds of Change is dedicated to spreading the practices of sustainable agriculture worldwide by preserving the plants and agricultural customs that are distinctive to particular places. They provide 100 percent organic, open-pollinated seeds grown primarily on their research farms in New Mexico and Oregon. Their products are available through their catalog, in natural food stores, and on their website. Contact: Seeds of Change, P.O. Box 15700, Santa Fe, NM 87506-5700; 888-762-7333; http://www.seedsofchange.com.

Seed Savers Exchange

Founded in 1975 by Kent and Diane Whealy on their Decorah, Iowa, farm, Seed Savers Exchange has become the most important grassroots movement for propagating and preserving heirloom seeds and educating people about the value of genetic and cultural diversity. Hundreds of varieties of vegetables and flowers are grown each year at SSE's Heritage Farm, but membership in this organization also introduces heirloom gardeners to likeminded enthusiasts who are interested in trading seeds—and stories—from their own homegrown supply. Contact Seed Savers Exchange, 3094 North Winn Road, Decorah, IA, 52101; 563-382-5990; http://www.seedsavers.org.

Sobel, David. *Place-Based Education: Connecting Classrooms and Communities.* Nature Literacy Series, vol. 4. Great Barrington, MA: Orion Society, 2004.

Sobel is a director of education at Antioch New England Graduate School and an ardent proponent of connecting people's education with the places they live. In contrast to the globalizing tendencies of much of higher education these days, place-based teaching begins by affirming the fundamental human need for a sense of place and proceeds by asking questions and telling stories about the local community in order to engender what Sobel calls "an enlightened localism." This book provides insights into what a place-based approach to Christian education might look like. See also Sobel's other titles: *Beyond Ecophobia: Reclaiming the Heart in Nature Education* (Great Barrington, MA: Orion Society, 2005), and *Mapmaking with Children: Sense of Place Education for the Elementary Years* (Portsmouth, NH: Heinemann, 1998).

Weaver, William Woys. *Heirloom Vegetable Gardening*. New York: Henry Holt, 1997.

Complete with beautiful photographs of rare heirlooms, Weaver's book is a treasure trove of information on vegetables that were once abundant in farmers' markets across the country but are now in danger of being lost entirely. He includes tips on planting, seed saving, and fascinating historical information about each of the varieties he features. If this book does not inspire you to become an heirloom vegetable gardener, nothing will.